The Expository Pulpit Series

JAMES

Faith In Action

BY

DR. GLEN E. SPENCER JR.

Dr. Glen E. Spencer Jr.
15 Pine Ridge Road – Tunkhannock, Pa. 18657
Email: PastorGlenSpencer@gmail.com

James: Faith In Action

Copyright © 2008 by Glen Spencer Jr.

All Rights Reserved. No part of this book may be reproduced, stored in a retrieval system or transmitted in any form by any means, electronic, mechanical, photocopy, recording, or otherwise, without the prior permission of the author, except as provided by USA copyright law.

All Scripture Quotations From The King James Bible

Contents

Coming Out On Top Of Your Trials 7

The Truth About Temptation 29

The Believer And The Bible 45

Everybody Is Somebody In God's House 63

Faith That Works 77

Don't Get Hung By Your Tongue 89

The Importance Of Heavenly Wisdom 101

Worldly Conflict In God's House 115

Failing To Put God Into Your Plans 133

Wealth, Wages and Wrath 139

Enduring With Patience 149

Prayer For The Hurting 161

Restoring The Wayward 183

Recommendations From Our Readers

Pastor Spencer is not only a gifted preacher, but a gifted writer as well. As a fundamentalist and pastor, I am careful about the books I endorse, but Dr. Spencer is at the top of my list of writers. So, it is with great honor that I recommend his Expository Pulpit Series to you.

Michael D. McClary, Th.D,

Pastor, Community-Bainbridge Baptist Church,

Founder/Executive Director, Good Samaritan Ministries

I have enjoyed reading your books in the past and look forward to getting newer ones. The thing I enjoyed about your books were that when I read them I said, "I have to teach this to my people. I want others to know this". I appreciate your study, work and insight.

Dr. Jeff Fugate

Pastor, Clays Mill Road Baptist Church

President of Commonwealth Baptist College

Dr. Glen Spencer's Bible commentaries are valuable for today. They are expository, edifying and exciting in aiding the Christian, the teacher and the preacher to understand the mind of God and to become victorious in their daily lives. I will use the complete set.

Dr. Bruce Miller, Evangelist

President of Atlantic Coast Baptist College

It is with great delight that I recommend to you, "The Expository Pulpit Commentary Series." Dr. Glen Spencer Jr. combines years of exhaustive research and practical ministry experience to bring to the church, the pastor, the teacher, and the student of the Scriptures a sound, in-depth and yet very practical set of study tools. This ongoing verse by commentary series will be a great addition to your library. This is not just more rehashed information but wise insight from a seasoned Bible Scholar. I know Dr. Glen Spencer Jr. the man and have found him to be a great Christian, a compassionate pastor and a true champion of the authorized King James Bible, believing it to be God's Preserved Word For English speaking people.

This trustworthy commentary series is, Dispensational in theology, pre-Tribulation and pre-millennial in its eschatology, literal in its hermeneutical approach and expository in its format. I am thrilled that this good work is now available to you and I as we seek to benefit from its invaluable help to deepen our knowledge of God's perfect, preserved word.

Dr. Jon M. Jenkins,

Pastor, Grace Baptist Church

President of Grace Baptist College

You have written an excellent study on the Book of Revelation. This will be a great help to preachers and teachers everywhere. This work is informative, inspiring, and encouraging. Your alliterative outlines are excellent! Your study of this book will be a great help to many, many Christians.

Dr. Lee Roberson

Founder of Tennessee Temple University

Coming Out On Top Of Your Trials

James 1:1-12

James, a servant of God and of the Lord Jesus Christ... (James 1:1) There is humility in this statement. James was the half-brother of Jesus Christ, yet he identified himself as a **servant**. James made no claim to fame, he simply identified himself as a **servant**. The word for servant is *"doulos"* and carries the idea of being dedicated to the will and service of another. James was devoted to Jesus to the disregard of his own interests.

Being a servant of Christ changes the way we look at trials. How many times have you faced trials and thought It just can't get any worse than this. Well, it can get worse. The fact of the matter is we are going to have to face many trials as we tread this pilgrim pathway. James addresses his letter to the **twelve tribes which are scattered abroad. (James 1:1)** The two words **scattered abroad** comes from the word *"diaspora"* and carries the idea of *"that which is sown."* It was a word used of the farmer sowing seed in the field. It was a term understood by Jews to speak of those who had been scattered abroad through persecution. Like a farmer sows seed in his field, the Lord sows Christians throughout the fields of this world.

In the book of Acts God allowed persecution to scatter His people for purpose of spreading the good news of the gospel. Think about it! You are where you are because God has put you there to spread the gospel.

The Christians from the twelve tribes were scattered because of the intense persecution that befell those who identified with Christ. Embracing Christ as Saviour immediately resulted in trials for the early believers. In this letter James tells them and us how to handle the trails of life and not only how to handle them, but how to come out on top.

THERE IS A PROPER ATTITUDE

My brethren, count it all joy when ye fall into divers temptations; Knowing this, that the trying of your faith worketh patience. But let patience have her perfect work, that ye may be perfect and entire, wanting nothing. (James 1:2-4) The right attitude is essential to the Christian life. Attitude determines atmosphere. If your attitude stinks, your life will stink.

> **For as he thinketh in his heart, so is he ... (Proverbs 23:7a)**

It is absolutely necessary that we think right when it comes to this matter of trials. In these two verses James gives us a four-fold attitude that we ought to have in dealing with our trials.

EXPECT YOUR TRIALS

Notice that James does not say IF, but WHEN ye fall into divers temptations. The word temptation is used two different ways in the Bible. The word is used speaking of a solicitation to sin as in 1 Timothy 6:9. But the word is also used a second way to describe the outward afflictions that we have in the world. Paul testified that he had served the Lord with all humility of mind, and with many tears, and temptations, which befell me by the lying in wait of the Jews: (Acts 20:19) Here Paul uses the word temptations to describe the outward affliction and persecutions that he faced as he served Christ. Now the second usage is what James means here when he speaks of divers temptations. In his book, *"The Secret of Christian Joy,"* Vance Havner said:

> "Let it not be forgotten that a twice-born and Spirit-filled Christian is always a contradiction to this old world. He

crosses it at every point. From the day that he is born again until he passes on to be with the Lord, he pulls against the current of a world forever going the other way. The real firebrand is distressing to the devil, and when a wide-awake believer comes along, taking the Gospel seriously, we can expect sinister maneuvering for his downfall."

The child of God will face trials in this life. The Christian life is not always smooth sailing. Any believer who is committed to living for the Lord will soon face opposition. We are to expect it! Peter agreed with James. He said:

Beloved, think it not strange concerning the fiery trial which is to try you, as though some strange thing happened unto you. (1 Peter 4:12)

Paul said:

We are troubled on every side ... (2 Corinthians 4:8)

Trials are not uncommon to the believer. We can expect them.

ENJOY YOUR TRIALS

James says, **count it all joy.** James ties our trials and our joy together. These are terms that we would not normally put together. Joy is not the natural human response to trouble. The flesh rejects trouble. But these were not flesh driven believers. These are people who walked with the Lord and because of their faith were suffering persecution. Jesus said that it would happen.

> **In the world ye shall have tribulation: but be of good cheer; I have overcome the world. (John 16:33)**

Paul warned:

> **Yea, and all that will live godly in Christ Jesus shall suffer persecution. (2 Timothy 3:12)**

The people to whom James writes had been driven from their homes, lost everything they owned, rejected by their families and James says, enjoy yourselves! Rejoice in your service to the Lord. Count it all joy brethren. We see the same thought in First Peter.

> **But rejoice, inasmuch as ye are partakers of Christ's sufferings; that, when his glory shall be revealed, ye may be glad also with exceeding joy. If ye be reproached for the name of Christ, happy are ye; for the spirit of glory and of God resteth upon you: on their part he is evil spoken of, but on your part he is glorified. (1 Peter 4:13-14)**

Peter is talking about suffering here and he speaks in terms such as **rejoice, be glad also with exceeding joy,** and **happy are ye.** These are terms that we wouldn't usually associate with suffering. However, James and Peter are teaching us that suffering results in joy when we have the proper attitude. When the Apostles were persecuted, the Bible says:

> **And they departed from the presence of the council rejoicing that they were counted worthy to suffer shame for his name. (Acts 5:41)**

When Paul and Silas were imprisoned for preaching Christ we are told that they **prayed and sang praises unto God: and the prisoners heard them (Acts 16:25).** Paul also said, **But we glory in tribulations (Romans 5:3).**

The reason for our rejoicing is that we have a different perspective. We are not self-centered, we are Christ-centered. The Christian life is not about us, it is about Him. Peter said we are:

> **... partakers of Christ's sufferings; that, when his glory shall be revealed, ye may be glad also with exceeding joy. (1 Peter 4:13)**

Notice that this is about revealing Christ's glory. The word **revealed** means to *"unveil, to uncover, to cause something to be known."* Our suffering is designed to reveal Christ in our lives. If I handle suffering right, Christ is revealed to all those around me.

> **For I reckon that the sufferings of this present time are not worthy to be compared with the glory which shall be revealed in us. (Romans 8:18)**

We should also take note of the fact that Peter didn't just say joy, but **ALL joy**. This is the degree to which we are to joy. The word **all** carries the idea of *"all the way."* Instead of complaining about our troubles, we rejoice in them for they offer an opportunity to testify of Christ's power and goodness. The teaching here is simple. As God's children we are not to divide life into the enjoyable and miserable. Instead we are to enjoy **all** of life.

Evaluate Your Trials

James uses the word **count** here to teach us a very important lesson. The word **count** is an accounting term. It speaks of calculating interest. When you make an investment you calculate the interest to evaluate what your earnings are going to be. That is the word James uses in connection with our trials. The investment produces earnings. Therefore, look at the positive side of the ledger. There is a profit to be gained.

When Jesus took his disciples over the Sea of Galilee, He took them right through a dreadful storm. It was a trying experience for the disciples, but there was great opportunity for ministry awaiting them. When they arrived safely on the other side they freed a Demoniac Man, healed a Diseased Woman and raised a Dead Girl. That's ministry! But they had to pass through a great trial to get there.

Think about Joseph. His life seemed to be one disappointment after the other. At seventeen years of age, he was ripped away from home and family, sold to a bunch of ruthless peddlers, taken to a foreign country, put on the slave block and resold only to become a common slave. His owners wife lied about him and framed him for something he didn't do and off to prison he goes. By man's standards Joseph should have been eaten up with a vile bitterness that would have ruined his life. But instead of getting bitter, Joseph counted it all joy as he endured the trials of life.

Later as Joseph spoke to his brothers about their offense, he said:

> *But as for you, ye thought evil against me; but God meant it unto good, to bring to pass, as it is this day, to save much people alive. (Genesis 50:20)*

Joseph's focus was always a heavenly one. This was the philosophy that permeated Joseph's life. He fully relied upon the living God and trusted Him completely.

He realized that God providentially ordered all the events of his life. W. H. Griffith-Thomas wrote:

> *"Happy is the man whose eye is open to see the hand of God in everyday events, for to him life always possesses a wonderful and true joy and glory."*

If we handle our trials the way Joseph handled his, we will come out on top.

ENDURE YOUR TRIALS

Knowing this, that the trying of your faith worketh patience. But let patience have her perfect work, that ye may be perfect and entire, wanting nothing. (James 1:3-4) Here we are told that trials have a definite purpose. **Trying** is a word that speaks of the process of refining precious metals. Peter used the same analogy.

> **That the trial of your faith, being much more precious than of gold that perisheth, though it be tried with fire. (1 Peter 1:7a)**

For raw gold to be purified it must be melted and the dross skimmed off. In order to do that the gold must be heated to 1,900 degrees Fahrenheit. Once the gold is melted, the impurities rise to the surface, where they are skimmed off. God does the same thing with our faith. He allows our faith to enter into the fire. He allows these trials and afflictions into our lives for the purpose of burning off the impurities and leaving us with pure, genuine faith. David said:

> **For thou, O God, hast proved us: thou hast tried us, as silver is tried. (Psalms 66:10)**

For the Christian a trial is the hand of God at work in our life. We simply need to accept trials as a normal part of the Christian life.

James says that this trying of our faith **worketh patience.** The word **patience** comes from two words, *"hupo"* meaning *"under"* and *"mone"* meaning *"abide."* So the word literally means *to abide under.* The word was used of a donkey remaining steady under his load. Instead of giving up, he bears up under the load. James uses the same word when he speaks of **the patience of Job. (James 5:11)** Job serves as an illustration of bearing up under a load. Paul said:

> **And let us not be weary in well doing: for in due season we shall reap, if we faint not. (Galatians 6:9)**

That word **faint** is the opposite of patience. It means to become weary and give up. God's people are not to be quitters. We bear up as God strengthens us and we move forward. These trials actually condition and strengthen us so that we will be able to bear up under the next trial.

The word **worketh** carries the idea of *"fully accomplishing something."* The idea is to work out, to accomplish, to do something thoroughly. Trials thoroughly produce a faith that results in persistence. The test of one area of our lives produces power in another area.

THERE IS A PRESCRIBED APPROACH

We have to learn how to deal with our trials. This is where a lot of folks mess up. If we fail to draw upon God's resources our trials will overcome us wreck our joy. James offers two important points on how to approach the problems of life.

WE MUST ACQUIRE WISDOM

If any of you lack wisdom, let him ask of God, that giveth to all men liberally, and upbraideth not; and it shall be given him. (James 1:5) In the midst of life's trials we need wisdom. We have just been instructed to **count it all joy** when we face our trials. We learned that the word **count** speaks of calculating our earnings. There is a profit to be gained in our trials if we handle them right. Roy Laurin said:

> *"The permissive will of God allows situations to arise in our lives that may hurt us, but it is only to help us. There is*

some dividend in every difficulty. The smart man is the one who is wise enough to compel his difficulty to pay him that dividend."

To earn dividends from our trials we need wisdom. Not just any wisdom, but Divine wisdom. Any fool can endure suffering, but it takes wisdom to turn trials into a profit. Solomon said:

Wisdom is the principal thing; therefore get wisdom: and with all thy getting get understanding. (Proverbs 4:7)

Wisdom is the correct use of knowledge. It is the ability to exercise the discernment and judgment of God's Word. Wisdom is the ability to apply the Bible to our everyday life. Every child of God needs His wisdom.

The word **lack** is a banking term that speaks of falling short in one's account. A lot of times we fall short on wisdom. Where are we going to get such wisdom? James says that we are to **ask of God. (James 1:5)** It is tragic that so many people turn everywhere except to the source of all true wisdom! James does not say, If any of you lack wisdom, go to the university. Neither does he say, Go to the philosophers. We are not instructed to get the latest Best Seller. But he says, **Let him ask of God.** James speaks of two kinds of wisdom. In chapter three he talks about wisdom that **descendeth not from above… (James 3:15)** He also talks about a wisdom **that is from above. (James 3:17)** God wants us to be wise and He has made it possible for us to have wisdom. All we have to do is **ask of God.** Keep in mind that this is James speaking about prayer here. James had spent so much time on his knees praying that they were covered with big calluses. He was called Old Camel Knees. James speaks with authority—as one who well knew of God's willingness to answer prayer.

And look at the promise! God **giveth to all men.** Not some men, but all men. Every child of God can have wisdom. The humblest believer can have this Divine wisdom. He may be uneducated. He may be poor. He may be a little rough around the edges, but he can be wise if he will seek God's face. There is no excuse for foolishness. Notice that there are no conditions attached to this promise. There are many things for which we pray that we must say *"If it be Thy will."* But when it comes to wisdom the Bible is clear, God **giveth to all men** if they will ask. We can have wisdom.

James goes on to say that God **giveth to all men liberally, and upbraideth not.** You remember how that God appeared to Solomon and said:

> **Ask what I shall give thee. (2 Chronicles 1:7)**

Think about that! Solomon could ask anything of the Lord and get it. Solomon said to the Lord.

> **Give me now wisdom and knowledge ... (2 Chronicles 1:10)**

Now look at God's response.

> **And God said to Solomon, Because this was in thine heart, and thou hast not asked riches, wealth, or honour, nor the life of thine enemies, neither yet hast asked long life; but hast asked wisdom and knowledge for thyself, that thou mayest judge my people, over whom I have made thee king: Wisdom and knowledge is granted unto thee; and I will give thee riches, and wealth, and honour, such as none of the kings have had that have been before thee, neither shall there any after thee have the like. (2 Chronicles 1:11-12)**

God not only gives, He gives **liberally**. Matthew Poole said that God gives:

> *"... with an open, free, large heart, in opposition to the contracted, narrow spirits of covetous misers."*

Such is how God gives wisdom. There is no reason for any Christian to be lacking in Heavenly wisdom (Proverbs 1:20).

WE MUST AVOID WAVERING

But let him ask in faith, nothing wavering. (James 1:6a) In order to receive this wisdom from God we must ask in faith. We must believe that He is able to give, and that He is willing to give, and that He will give. Faith is simply taking God at His word and acting upon it. Faith moves the heart of God.

But without faith it is impossible to please him: for he that cometh to God must believe that he is, and that he is a rewarder of them that diligently seek him. (Hebrews 11:6)

The idea of praying with faith is that of approaching God as credible and One who keeps His promises. He is trustworthy! He said He would give us the wisdom. Therefore, we ask for it believing that He will deliver. Faith is reliance on the character and genuineness of God's promises.

For he that wavereth is like a wave of the sea driven with the wind and tossed. For let not that man think that he shall receive any thing of the Lord. A double minded man is unstable in all his ways. (James 1:6b-8) It must be pure faith with no mixture of doubting. Paul said:

> **I will therefore that men pray every where, lifting up holy hands, without wrath and doubting. (1 Timothy 2:8)**

James compares the doubter to the restless wave that dashes against the rocks on the shore. Nothing is accomplished by its activity. Believing prayer rests its confidence in God, but doubt exhibits a lack of confidence in Him and results in an unstable, frustrating life.

THERE IS A PERILOUS APPEARANCE

One of our problems is that we often judge based on outward appearances. Many have a tendency to disregard the man of **low degree** while honoring the **rich man**. The fellow with money and a high social standing is usually preferred over the fellow who has little of the world's riches. This can be a big problem when facing trials. We have to realize that the man who has money faces trials the same as a man with no money.

APPEARANCE AND POVERTY

Let the brother of low degree rejoice in that he is exalted: (James 1:9) The phrase **low degree** describes one who is low on the social and economic scale. It speaks of one who lives in very humble conditions, someone who is very poor. Poverty was a major trial facing these dispersed Christians. They had to leave their jobs, their homes, their families and were scattered around the country with little more than the clothes on their back. Nothing seems to cause divided loyalties between a man and God quite like money. The lack of finances is a great hindrances to the ministry. It is hard to mind the things of God when the bills aren't paid. Oh I know! Someone is thinking. *"Well we have to live by faith."* I'm all for living by faith. But just try going to the grocery store, loading your cart, and telling the store manager that you are taking the groceries home without paying for them. Your faith will have no bearing on the grocer whatsoever. The bottom line is we need money to make it in this world and Satan knows how to use a Christian's finances to discourage him.

We live in a society where money talks. So the brother of **low degree** wouldn't mean much to the world. However, to God he is of great value. So much so that James says **rejoice in that he is exalted.** We may not mean much to the higher ups of society, but God has exalted him. We have been adopted into the family of God. This is a principle of the Christian life.

> **But many that are first shall be last; and the last shall be first. (Matthew 19:30)**

Some of the big shots are going to be last when we get to Heaven. The idea behind the word **rejoice** is that of *"boasting and bragging."* When James says **Let**

the brother of low degree rejoice in that he is exalted, He is saying *"You've got something to be proud of in that you are a child of God, boast about it."* What a position!

As followers of Christ we belong to a Heavenly realm. We are not beggars. We are of great worth to God! We are His children and we should rejoice because we have:

> **... an inheritance incorruptible, and undefiled, and that fadeth not away, reserved in heaven... (1 Peter 1:4)**

Jim Elliot said:

> *"He is no fool who gives what he cannot keep to gain what he cannot lose."*

Money might be tight and we may not have the best of houses but Jesus made it clear that:

> **...a man's life consisteth not in the abundance of the things which he possesseth. (Luke 12:15)**

Rather than dealing with our trials by focusing on our lack let us be thankful for all that we do have in Christ.

APPEARANCE AND PROSPERITY

But the rich, in that he is made low: because as the flower of the grass he shall pass away. For the

sun is no sooner risen with a burning heat, but it withereth the grass, and the flower thereof falleth, and the grace of the fashion of it perisheth: so also shall the rich man fade away in his ways. (James 1:10-11) James now addresses Christians who had money. There were many such people in the early Church. There were men like Joseph of Arimathaea, Nicodemus, and Barnabas. There were people of means who were born and raised in the lap of luxury. Others have worked hard and built their fortunes from scratch. However, one thing that is usually true of those who have wealth is that they live a better quality of life than those without money. If a man with money is not careful he will tend to trust in his finances. Guy King said of the rich man:

> *"He is apt to judge life, and to measure his fellows, by the yard-stick of finance. Yet, in his capacity as a rich man, he is really no more stable than the grass; the burning heat of some sudden calamity, of some unexpected movement of the money-market, reduces him to the mere ashes of his former self."*

The Word of God warns us to …

> **… be not highminded, nor trust in uncertain riches, but in the living God, who giveth us richly all things to enjoy; (1 Timothy 6:17)**

Pride and riches often go together. The rich man must keep the proper perspective on money. James says, the rich man is to rejoice in that **he is made low.** Notice James does not tell the rich man to rejoice because of his riches; rather, he tells him to rejoice because he has realized his spiritual poverty and trusted Christ for salvation. The poor man is exalted and the rich man is made low. The idea is that our relationship with Christ brings us to the same level. Regardless of our financial worth, our abilities or anything else we may be, we need to avoid the allusions of the world and realize what we have in Christ.

THERE IS A PLEASANT ACCOMPLISHMENT

Blessed is the man that endureth temptation: for when he is tried, he shall receive the crown of life, which the Lord hath promised to them that love him. (James 1:12) James says, **Blessed is the man that endureth temptation.** The word **blessed** simply means *"happy."* The happy man is not the man who does not have trials, but the man who **endureth temptation.** The word **endureth** comes from the Greek *"hypomeno"* and means *"to remain, stay the course, tarry."* It describes staying the course regardless of trials and troubles. Someone has well said, "Quitters Never Win And Winners Never Quit." There are blessings associated with our troubles. This may seem a little strange at first thought. However, when we think about it, it is not strange; for we know that trials and tribulations build character and makes us stronger. Many a ministry has flourished in the fire of affliction. The Puritan Richard Baxter said it well:

> "Afflictions are God's most effectual means to keep us from losing our way to our heavenly rest. Without this hedge of thorns on the right and left we should hardly keep the way to heaven. If there be but one gap open, how ready are we to find it and turn out at it. When we grow wanton, or worldly, or proud, how doth sickness or other affliction reduce us! Every Christian, as well as Luther, may call affliction one of his best schoolmasters, and with David may say, Before I was afflicted I went astray, but now have I kept thy word. Many thousand recovered sinners may cry, O healthful sickness! O comfortable sorrows! O gainful hope! O enriching poverty! Oh blessed day that ever I was afflicted! Not only the green pastures and still waters, but the rod and staff, they comfort us."

James goes on to say, ... **for when he is tried, he shall receive the crown of life, which the Lord hath promised to them that love him. (James 1:12b)**

Christians do have trials. Praise God, for He has promised us that:

> *... all things work together for good to them that love God, to them who are the called according to his purpose. (Romans 8:28)*

However, we have the blessed promise of Scripture that our trials are designed by the Lord for our own good in conforming us to the image of His Dear Son.

The Truth About Temptation

James 1:13-17

James now shifts from trials to temptations. Trials can come from God, but temptation can never come from Him. A trial is difficulty or trouble that comes from God for the purpose of building us up in the faith. A temptation is a solicitation to sin that comes from Satan for the purpose of ruining our walk with God. You will remember that after Abraham obeyed God and left Ur, a famine fell upon the land (Genesis 12:10). He stepped out on faith and the thing to do would be to continue in faith. Instead he went down to Egypt for food. While he was there he lied about Sarah being his sister (Genesis 12:11-13). As a result of Abraham's lack of faith and lying, the King was tempted to take Sarah as his wife. Abraham was consequently thrown out of Egypt (Genesis 12:19-20). This famine was a trial from God. But the idea of going to Egypt was a temptation from Satan. It is necessary that we learn to distinguish between trials and temptations. We need to make sure a trial from God is not turned into a temptation to evil by Satan. There are three main points that stand out in this passage.

THE REALITY OF TEMPTATION

Let no man say when he is tempted, I am tempted of God: for cannot be tempted with evil, neither tempteth he any man: (James 1:13) James makes it clear that God is not the source of our temptation. When temptation to sin comes our way we are not to blame God for it. **God cannot be tempted with evil, neither tempteth he any man.** God's desire is to salvage man from his sin, not cause him to sin. Yet many people blame God for their own sin and failure. They say, *"God created me like this. God gave me these desires."* This argument is often used by the adulterer and the sodomite. On and on they go as they attempt to justify and rationalize their sin. Their reasoning concludes that God is the author of sin. What a vain and blasphemous claim.

This was the thinking behind Adam's wretched attempt to shift the responsibility for his sin. God came to the garden in the cool of the day and calls out to Adam, **Where art thou? (Genesis 3:9)** Adam answered:

> **I heard thy voice in the garden, and I was afraid, because I was naked; and I hid myself. And he said, Who told thee**

> that thou wast naked? Hast thou eaten of the tree, whereof I commanded thee that thou shouldest not eat? (Genesis 3:10-11)

Neither of God's questions required a detailed explanation. All Adam really had to do was say, Yes, I did eat of the forbidden tree. But notice Adam's reply,

> **The woman whom thou gavest to be with me, she gave me of the tree, and I did eat. (Genesis 3:12)**

Adam's reply was nothing more than a feeble attempt to shift the blame for his sin onto his wife Eve. And notice that he wasn't just blaming Eve, but when he said, **the woman whom thou gavest to be with me,** he was blaming God. His insinuation was *Lord am in this mess because of you.* "If you hadn't given me that woman, I never would have sinned." There is a propensity in us to find excuses for our sin. Eve did the same thing.

> **And the LORD God said unto the woman, What is this that thou hast done? And the woman said, The serpent beguiled me, and I did eat. (Genesis 3:13)**

Rather than admitting that she had disobeyed the Lord, she played the blame game. Some stumble over this whole account of Adam and Eve in Eden. I've even heard folks come right out and say that God is responsible for their sin because He put the tree of the knowledge of good and evil there and forbad them to eat of it. Their claim is that God was cause of Eve's temptation. However, it must be understood that the tree was not to be a solicitation to evil, but rather as a point of proving their faith and obedience. Dr. Lehman Strauss wrote:

> *"The one restriction that God had placed upon our first parents was reasonable, being a test of their faith and obedience, not a temptation to do wrong. The power of choice lay with them, and they had as much power to choose the good as they had to choose the evil. God did not compel Adam and Eve to eat the fruit; He forbade them, and yet Adam sought to blame the Lord."*

God will test us, but He will never tempt us to do evil. Someone has said, *"God may test you to strengthen your faith, but He never tempts you to subvert your faith."* The New Bible Dictionary explains:

> *Satan test's God's people, by manipulating circumstances, within the limits that God allows him in an attempt to make them desert God's will. (Job 1:12 2:6 1 Corinthian 10:13).*

God is not the agent of temptation. Eve fell into sin because she fell for Satan's manipulation of the truth. Both Adam and Eve tried to pass the blame for their sin, but it didn't work. From the Garden of Eden to the present day, folks have always tried to dodge their personal responsibility for sin. Adam said, *"It's not my fault! The woman made me do it."* Eve said, *"It's not my fault! The devil made me do it."* But they were held accountable for their sin and when it comes to our sin, so will we. Every person will stand before God at the judgment and answer for his or her sin.

> **For God shall bring every work into judgment, with every secret thing, whether it be good or whether it be evil. (Ecclesiastes 12:14)**

A few verses down, James reiterates the fact that God does not solicit us to evil. **Every good gift and every perfect gift is from above, and cometh down from the Father of lights, with whom is no variableness, neither shadow of turning. (James 1:17)** The word **gift** signifies the act of giving. The emphasis is on the Giver. The idea here is that nothing bad comes from God. Only good gifts come from our Heavenly Father. Those who blame God for their temptation need to develop a Biblical understanding about the nature of God. The worst mistake we could make is to misunderstand the nature of God to the point that we blame Him for evil.

James describes God as the **Father of lights**. This is a reference to God as Creator of the heavenly bodies such as the sun, the moon, and the stars.

> **To him that made great lights: for his mercy endureth for ever: The sun to rule by day: for his mercy endureth for ever: The moon and stars to rule by night: for his mercy endureth for ever. (Psalms 136:7-9)**

God is Light. Light speaks of His pure character. The Bible says, **God is light, and in him is no darkness at all. (1 John 1:5b)** The fact that God created the sun and the stars to give us light proves that He is a good God who gives good gifts. On the day of creation the Bible says, **And God saw the light, that it was good …** When God was finished with creation the Bible says, **And God saw every thing that he had made, and, behold, it was very good …** God's goodness is demonstrated in His creation.

James goes on to assure us that God's goodness will never change. He will always be good. God is the **with whom is no variableness, neither shadow of turning. (James 1:17b)** The word **variableness** carries the idea of fickleness or variation. The phrase **shadow of turning** describes a shadow that is cast by the turning of an object. God does not vary in His nature. There will never be a shadow that passes over God's character. This speaks of God's immutability.

Immutability is the Divine attribute of being unchangeable. It means that God does not change. His character is forever set. God is therefore utterly dependable. **For I am the LORD, I change not … (Malachi 3:6a)** God is absolutely unchangeable. He will always be good.

THE ROUTE OF TEMPTATION

Now, James lays out the course of temptation. Satan is a wise enemy. He knows well how to conquer man. Here we see that temptation Commences with Desire, Continues with Deception and Concludes with Death.

COMMENCES WITH DESIRE

But every man is tempted … of his own lust … (James 1:14) This gets right down to bare facts. The main problem we have is that of our own sinful flesh. Satan knows how to effectively use the lusts and desires that already reside in the heart. Though the believer has received a new nature—a **divine nature (2 Peter 1:4),** we are nevertheless hounded by the flesh. It is a nature of depravity and corruption and delights in sin and wickedness.

The Bible sometimes refers to this old nature as the **old man.** Paul speaking to the Ephesian Church admonished them to deal with the flesh.

> **That ye put off concerning the former conversation the old man, which is**

> **corrupt according to the deceitful lusts. (Ephesians 4:22)**

These were born again, blood washed children of God that Paul was talking to. But notice that he admonished them to put off the **old man.** The sin nature wasn't gone. It was still there and had to be dealt with according to the Word of God. There are three truths that stand out in the Word of God concerning the old nature. When it comes to the flesh, there will be …

First, **<u>No Rest</u>**. A Spirit-filled believer will never be at peace with the old man. **For the flesh lusteth against the Spirit, and the Spirit against the flesh: and these are contrary the one to the other: so that ye cannot do the things that ye would. (Galatians 5:17)** The word **lusteth** speaks of a strong desire. Paul states that the Spirit and the flesh lust **against** each other, meaning they have opposite desires for us. The flesh wants us to succumb to sin while the Spirit wants us to live for Christ. Paul goes on to say that **these are contrary the one to the other.** The word **contrary** means to *"oppose or confront."* Here is the reason for the conflict that Christians have in their life as they struggle to put off the old and put on the new. The flesh dictates that we be one way and the Spirit immediately steps up and opposes the sinful nature and demands that we walk in the Spirit. The same word used here for **contrary** is translated *adversaries* in Luke 13:17 and 1 Corinthians 16:9. An adversary is an enemy or a foe. The flesh and the Spirit are adversaries—they are enemies and completely opposed to one another. They are not going to compromise and will never be at peace. The battle rages as these two adversaries fight to gain ground in the Christian's life.

Second, **No Righteousness**. You will never get anything good out of the old nature. It is a nature that is an enemy of God and hates everything that is holy and decent. **Paul said:**

> **For I know that in me (that is, in my flesh,) dwelleth no good thing: for to will is present with me; but how to perform that which is good I find not. (Romans 7:18)**

It was the old depraved nature that Jeremiah so vividly described when he said:

> **The heart is deceitful above all things, and desperately wicked: who can know it? (Jeremiah 17:9)**

Jesus put it this way:

> **That which cometh out of the man, that defileth the man. For from within, out of the heart of men, proceed evil thoughts, adulteries, fornications, murders, Thefts, covetousness,**

> wickedness, deceit, lasciviousness, an evil eye, blasphemy, pride, foolishness: All these evil things come from within, and defile the man. (Mark 7:20-23)

In Galatians we find a list of the fruit produced by the old nature.

> Now the works of the flesh are manifest, which are these; Adultery, fornication, uncleanness, lasciviousness, Idolatry, witchcraft, hatred, variance, emulations, wrath, strife, seditions, heresies, Envyings, murders, drunkenness, revellings, and such like: of the which I tell you before, as I have also told you in time past, that they which do such things shall not inherit the kingdom of God. (Galatians 5:19-21)

No wonder the Bible says:

> But we are all as an unclean thing, and all our righteousnesses are as filthy rags; and we all do fade as a leaf; and our iniquities, like the wind, have taken us away. (Isaiah 64:6)

Think about that! Even good works when accomplished in the flesh are unacceptable to God. The bottom line is that the flesh is incapable of producing anything that would please God. Jesus said, **the flesh profiteth nothing ... (John 6:63)** The doesn't profit a little, but **nothing**. The flesh cannot be used to the glory of Gid.

Third, **No Reform**. It is impossible to reform the flesh for it wants nothing to do with holiness and the things of God.

> **Because the carnal mind is enmity against God: for it is not subject to the law of God, neither indeed can be. (Romans 8:7)**

The old man can be crucified and controlled, but he cannot be reformed. The Bible tells us that the only method for dealing with the old nature is crucifixion. Paul said:

> **I am crucified with Christ: nevertheless I live; yet not I, but Christ liveth in me: and the life which I now live in the flesh I live by the faith of the Son of God, who loved me, and gave himself for me. (Galatians 2:20)**

Again, to the Romans, Paul wrote:

> **For if ye live after the flesh, ye shall die: but if ye through the Spirit do mortify the deeds of the body, ye shall live. (Romans 8:13)**

This is the believer's responsibility. If we are going to enjoy the victorious Christian life we absolutely must crucify the flesh.

> **And they that are Christ's have crucified the flesh with the affections and lusts. (Galatians 5:24)**

In the book of Romans Paul said:

> **Likewise reckon ye also yourselves to be dead indeed unto sin, but alive unto God through Jesus Christ our Lord. (Romans 6:12)**

Notice that we are to **reckon** our own selves dead. The word **reckon** means *"to count, to number and to calculate."* The idea is that of reconciling a checkbook. We take the bank statement and our checkbook, sit down and make the checkbook agree with the bank statement. That is what God is saying when He commands that we **reckon** ourselves to be dead. He has already declared it. The only thing left is for us to bring our life in line with His word. Reckoning is the step of faith that acknowledges what God says about me in the Bible is now true in my life. Again, there is no reform for the flesh—only death!

Please understand this! The old depraved nature that we battle with is indeed a powerful force. Most folks come into the Christian life with a lot of baggage and Satan knows how to use it against them. The lust, greed, anger, bitterness, and pride of man provides Satan a suitable workshop to use against us. **But every man is tempted ... of his own lust**. If the desire wasn't already in the heart, there wouldn't be a temptation. The reality is that we cannot blame anyone else. Man's sin problem comes from within himself.

CONTINUES WITH DECEPTION

But every man is tempted, when he is drawn away of his own lust, and enticed. (James 1:14) James uses two powerful illustrations here to describe the power of temptation. His first illustration comes from the world of hunting. He says that we are tempted, when we are **drawn away** by our lusts. The phrase **drawn away** speaks of using bait to draw an animal into the snare. Satan knows how to bait his traps well.

James' second illustration comes from the sport of fishing. The word **enticed** speaks of luring a fish to the hook. As a fisherman uses a lure to attract a fish, so our lust lures us into sin. Both of these illustrations vividly expresses the seductive nature of sin. The bait looks good to the rabbit and the lure looks good to the fish, but death is hidden in them. Life is full of hidden snares and baited hooks. Satan knows how to disguise sin. He has baited a lot of traps and he has cast a lot of lures—watch out for him.

James is telling us that it is our own lust that draws us into sin. James has dealt with both the desire and the deception. No one puts the snare around the rabbit's neck. He ends up snared because his own desire for the bait drew him into the trap. The same is true with fishing. No one put the lure in the fish's mouth. He was enticed and hooked because of his own desire to take the bait. Solomon said:

Keep thy heart with all diligence; for out of it are the issues of life. (Proverbs 4:23)

Mark this down! Sin never starts with the bait; it always starts with the desire of the heart. If the desire is not already active in the heart, the temptation will have no effect. We must guard against failure by staying in the Word and keeping our heart clean.

CONCLUDES WITH DEATH

Then when lust hath conceived, it bringeth forth sin: and sin, when it is finished, bringeth forth death. (James 1:15) Now James uses childbirth as an illustration of sin being conceived in the human heart. The word **conceived** means *"to bring together."* When a man and a woman come together a child is conceived. Like a baby in its mother's womb, sin is conceived and grows to maturity. However, new life is not the result of this conception. When lust conceives it gives birth to sin and when sin reaches its full development, it results in death. **The soul that sinneth ... (Ezekiel 18:20)**

The Response To Temptation

Do not err, my beloved brethren. (James 1:16) Here is a command not to sin. We do have a choice in the matter. We can say no to sin. We have already learned that God is good. Because He is good, He has given us a free will so that we can choose. He has also given us the Holy Spirit to help us make the right choice. Paul said:

> **This I say then, Walk in the Spirit, and ye shall not fulfil the lust of the flesh. (Galatians 5:16)**

What's more, God has promised us that He would make a way for us to escape.

> **There hath no temptation taken you but such as is common to man: but God is faithful, who will not suffer you to be tempted above that ye are able; but will with the temptation also make a way to escape, that ye may be able to bear it. (1 Corinthians 10:13)**

We don't have to make a shipwreck of our faith. Here is a promise that God will not allow us to be tempted above what we can handle. That means that God will limit the temptation to the point that we will not have to be overcome by it. That is a promise we can count on. The problem is that we sometime don't look for the escape.

It is important that we understand how the Sovereignty of God and the free will of man work together here. It is God who will make the way, but He makes it clear that we are to **bear it.** The ability to overcome is given by God, the act of overcoming is up to us—it is our decision.

> **Blessed is the man that endureth temptation: for when he is tried, he shall receive the crown of life, which the Lord hath promised to them that love him. (James 1:12)**

The Believer And The Bible

James 1:18-27

James deals with the believer's relationship to the Word of God. We live in a world that is Biblically illiterate. While we might expect such ignorance from the world, we must not expect or accept it from God's people. Too many professing Christians are just as ignorant concerning God's word as the world is. God's people are to be a people of the Bible. This simply cannot be. How the world ever receive Christ if believers are not apt to teach them about Christ. We must **_Learn_** the Bible, **_Love_** the Bible and **_Live_** the Bible. No other book in the world will do for us what the Bible will do.

Reality Of Conversion

James first deals with the priority of God's Word in relation to our salvation. Salvation begins and continues with the word of God. Apart from it there is no salvation, no security, no strengthening and no service. The Bible is our final authority in all matters of faith and practice.

God's Will

Of his own will begat he us ... (James 1:18a) When man fell God willed to save him. Salvation had its beginning in God's love. **We love him, because he first loved us. (1 John 4:19)** The word will speaks of God's desire to save the lost. God's desire or will to save extends to every person.

> **The Lord is not slack concerning his promise, as some men count slackness; but is longsuffering to us-ward, not willing that any should perish, but that all should come to repentance. (2 Peter 3:9)**

Though God wills that every person be saved, the individual must recognize his need of a Saviour and turn to Christ for forgiveness. This is where man's freewill comes into play. Though God wills for all to be saved, many will refuse His gracious offer of salvation. Jesus said:

> **O Jerusalem, Jerusalem, thou that killest the prophets, and stonest them which are sent unto thee, how often would I have gathered thy children together, even as a hen gathereth her**

> **chickens under her wings, and ye would not! (Matthew 23:37)**

The stubborn Pharisees could have been saved but they refused. Jesus said, ye would not. They exercised their freewill and rejected God's will. Everyone is a candidate for salvation. However, it is absolutely necessary for an individual to exercise his will to trust Jesus Christ as his Saviour if he is to be saved. Although God wants everyone to be saved, no one will be saved unless he recognizes his need and trusts Jesus Christ as his Saviour.

> **For this is good and acceptable in the sight of God our Saviour; Who will have all men to be saved, and to come unto the knowledge of the truth. (1 Timothy 2:3-4)**

God's Word

James says, **begat he us with the word of truth… (James 1:18b)** A few verse later James says, **receive with meekness the engrafted word, which is able to save your souls. (James 1:21b)** There is no salvation apart from the word of God. This is one of the reasons that Satan hates the word of God. We are told that God **begat** us with the word of truth. The word begat means *"to be birthed."* It speaks of a new life being brought forth. Life can only be produced from something that is alive itself. The Bible is a living book.

> For the word of God is quick, and powerful, and sharper than any twoedged sword, piercing even to the dividing asunder of soul and spirit, and of the joints and marrow, and is a discerner of the thoughts and intents of the heart. (Hebrews 4:12)

The **word of God is quick.** The word **quick** means *alive.* No wonder Jesus said:

> ... the words that I speak unto you, they are spirit, and they are life. (John 6:63b)

Paul said to the Romans:

> So then faith cometh by hearing, and hearing by the word of God. (Romans 10:17)

In the letter to the Ephesians he spoke of their having trusted in Christ **after that ye heard the Word of truth, the Gospel of your salvation. (Ephesians 1:13)** Peter says we are…

> ... born again, not of corruptible seed, but of incorruptible, by the word of God, which liveth and abideth for ever. (1 Peter 1:23)

The Lord Jesus Christ said:

> **Verily, verily, I say unto you, He that heareth my word, and believeth on him that sent me, hath everlasting life, and shall not come into condemnation; but is passed from death unto life. (John 5:24)**

It cannot be overemphasized that the Bible is the Word of truth and that apart from it there is no salvation. All who come to Jesus Christ must come by means of what He has said in His Word.

GOD'S WORK

James said, **that we should be a kind of firstfruits of his creatures. (James 1:18c)** The phrase firstfruits is distinctly Jewish. You will remember that James addressed them earlier as the **twelve tribes which are scattered abroad. (James 1:1)** These were Jewish converts and James spoke in terms that they will quickly grasp. In the first month of the Jewish year, the Jews observed three Jewish Feasts.

1) ***The Feast Of The Passover.*** This took place on the 14th day of the month. It was designed to be a reminder of how God had delivered the Israelites from bondage and brought them out of slavery.

2) ***The Feast Of Unleavened Bread***. This feast began the day after Passover and lasted for a week, during which the Jews removed all of the leaven from the bread that they ate. This was a

remembrance of their separation from Egypt. God had delivered them and made them a people who were to be set apart and different from the rest of the world. ... **the LORD doth put a difference between the Egyptians and Israel. (Exodus 11:7)**

3) ***The Feast Of Firstfruits***. The Feast of Firstfruits was a celebration of the firstfruits of the barley harvest (Exodus 23:16; Leviticus 2:12). This feast took place on the first day of the week following Passover. On this day, the Israelite would bring the first sheaf of grain and present to the Lord. The priest took the sheaf of grain and waved it before the altar of the Lord as an expression of appreciation for His wonderful supply.

When James spoke of the believer being a kind of **firstfruits of his creatures,** the Jewish Christians well understood what he meant. Here is the significance. The Lord's acceptance of the firstfruits was a pledge on His part of a full harvest to come. Just like the firstfruits represented a bountiful crop to come. These first-century Christians were a pledge of a great harvest of saved people in the centuries to come.

Reception That Cleanses

The **wherefore** of verse 19 is in reference to the salvation of verse 18. When the Word of God is implanted in our hearts, it produces new life. James lists four characteristics of the new life.

READINESS TO HEAR

James admonishes the believer to be **swift to hear ... (James 1:19a)** The hearing here has to do with the Word of God. When someone is truly born again there is a readiness to receive the Word of God. You can tell a lot about someone by the way they respond to God's Word. Lots of folks have a bits and pieces mentality when it comes to preaching. They treat the Bible like a smorgasbord, accepting the bits and pieces that tickle their ears, but rejecting anything they don't like. They turn away their ears from the truth (2 Timothy 4:4). Paul said:

Despise not prophesyings. (1 Thessalonians 5:20)

The word prophesyings comes from a word that means *"to speak, proclaim publicly."* In the context it is referring to the public declaration of God's word—the preaching of the word. The word despise means *"to regard as nothing, to despise utterly, to treat with contempt, to bring to naught, treat with scorn."* The is a very strong word that means to act as if the message means nothing. The idea is not to discount and or scoff at the preaching of God's word. It is interesting that the Lord has just warned us not to quench the Spirit and He follows it up with despise not prophesyings. One of the sure ways to quench the Spirit of God is by despising the message and or the messenger of God. This is a tough command for the days in which we live. People do not want to hear the preaching of the word.

James admonishes us to be **swift to hear**. The word **swift** means to be *"prompt and ready."* The idea is to be on our toes lest we miss something. The word **hear** goes beyond just the sense of hearing and carries the idea of *"giving an audience to."* The Thessalonians were **swift to hear** the word.

> **For this cause also thank we God without ceasing, because, when ye received the word of God which ye heard of us, ye received it not as the word of men, but as it is in truth, the word of God, which effectually worketh also in you that believe. (1 Thessalonians 2:13)**

The word **received** speaks of an *"open reception."* It carries the idea of readily and warmly welcoming God's word into their heart. James uses the same word, **receive with meekness the engrafted word, which is able to save your souls. (James 1:21)** James calls it the **engrafted word.** This is a horticulture term meaning *"to implant."* This is the only time this word is used in entire New Testament and speaks of grafting a branch from one tree onto another tree. Praise God when people receive the word of God this way. It is only when it is received with a welcome heart that it can take root and produce fruit. David said:

> **I have rejoiced in the way of thy testimonies, as much as in all riches. (Psalms 119:14)**

Hunger for the Word is a clear sign that a person is saved and desires to know God intimately.

RESTRAINT IN SPEAKING

We must be **slow to speak ... (James 1:19b)** Some folks are so busy talking that they can't hear. The command **slow to speak** insists that we be silent until we have understood and applied the word of God. It is a demand that we restrain our tongue lest we spout off before our brain is in gear.

> **Seest thou a man that is hasty in his words? there is more hope of a fool than of him. (Proverbs 29:20)**

A lot of trouble can come from hasty words.

> **In the multitude of words there wanteth not sin ... (Proverbs 10:19)**

Where there is a big mouth there is no shortage of sin. A loose tongue and sin go hand in hand. Wisdom teaches us to hold our tongue. Solomon said:

> **He that hath knowledge spareth his words ... (Proverbs 17:27)**

A young man came to the great philosopher Socrates to be trained as an orator. In his first meeting with his teacher, he began to talk without stopping. When Socrates could get a word in, he said, Young man, I will have to charge you a double fee. A double fee? Why is that? I will have to teach you two sciences. First, how to hold your tongue, and then how to use it.

Reluctance In Anger

We are to be ... **slow to wrath: For the wrath of man worketh not the righteousness of God. (James 1:19-20)** Isn't it interesting that in the context of receiving the word of God, we are warned about anger. We have an anger epidemic today. There are a lot of folks who are wasting away with anger. They have allowed anger to fester and grow until they are eaten up with bitterness. The Church is full of such people. God have mercy on the preacher who says one word about their pet sin or pet doctrine. Instead of receiving the word of God they blow up and blow out. But little do they know that it is not over. One day they will stand before God and be held accountable for what they heard and the Bible declares:

> **A man of great wrath shall suffer punishment ... (Proverbs 19:19)**

Before you go off halfcocked and blowing off at the mouth because you don't like what the preacher said it would be good to practice the first two steps of this passage. *First*, be swift to hear; *second*, be slow to speak, then if you are going to get mad anyway remember the words of Christ:

Whosoever is angry with his brother without a cause shall be in danger of the judgment ... (Matthew 5:22)

For the wrath of man worketh not the righteousness of God. (James 1:19-20) James tells us why we are to be slow to wrath. Nothing good ever comes from anger.

He that is soon angry dealeth foolishly ... (Proverbs 14:17)

I have seen a lot of damage caused by unwise and angry people. The Bible says:

A fool's wrath is presently known ... (Proverbs 12:16)

The word **presently** carries the idea of "*immediately* or *at once.*" In other words, as soon as he is angry you know it because his mouth starts to run. And the sad thing about it is that there are usually some young believers and children that hear the foolishness and it places a stumbling stone before them.

The first guy we have recorded in Scripture who blew up over what God said was Cain. He got mad because God required a blood sacrifice for sin. As a result of his anger he murdered his brother Abel (Genesis 4:1-8). Things didn't work out too good for Cain. However, anger is a common response to the word of God. In Acts chapter five when the Apostles preached God's Word it angered the Sadducees and they were:

> **... filled with indignation. (Acts 5:17)**

A little later we read:

> **When they heard that, they were cut to the heart, and took counsel to slay them. (Acts 5:33)**

When they heard the truth **they were cut to the heart.** They couldn't handle the conviction so they set out to kill the messengers rather than submit to the message. The same thing happened in Acts seven when Stephen preached.

> **When they heard these things, they were cut to the heart, and they gnashed on him with their teeth. (Acts 7:54)**

Paul includes **wrath** as one of the works of the flesh (Galatians 5:20). He then warns us that wrath must be:

> **... put away. (Ephesians 4:31)**

The Word of God speaks of being slow to anger and the benefits of ruling the spirit.

> **He that is slow to anger is better than the mighty; and he that ruleth his spirit than he that taketh a city. (Proverbs 16:32)**

Anger is a dangerous demon. It is evident that anger has infiltrated and dominated our society! But what a sad fix we are in when God's people display anger and rejection rather than repentance when the word of God is preached.

RESISTANCE TO EVIL

Wherefore lay apart all filthiness and superfluity of naughtiness, and receive with meekness the engrafted word, which is able to save your souls. (James 1:21) The words **lay apart** means *"to put off or strip away."* The idea is of stripping away or taking off dirty clothes. **Superfluity** is a strong phrase that carries the idea of *"overflow, abundance or excess."* The word **naughtiness** means *"wickedness, moral defilement or impurity."* **Filthiness** comes from the greek *"rhyparia."* It is a compound word from which we get the word *"earwax."* Earwax has a great purpose. It keeps insects and dirt from penetrating the ear. But if it builds up too much it hinders our ability to hear. In the context James is talking about hearing and receiving the Word of God. James is illustrating the fact that filthiness in our lives will keep us from hearing the Word of God. Like earwax keeps sound from penetrating our ears, filthiness will keep the word of God from penetrating our hearts.

Reflection That Corrects

For if any be a hearer of the word, and not a doer, he is like unto a man beholding his natural face in a glass: For he beholdeth himself, and goeth his way, and straightway forgetteth what manner of man he was. (James 1:23-24) James uses the illustration of looking at our **natural face** in a mirror. The phrase **natural face** simply means *"the face one was born with."* If it's ugly, it's ugly. If it's nice, praise the Lord. But whatever it is, it is what you have and you're stuck with it. And when you look in a mirror you see exactly what you have to deal with. Some require a bit of work. Someone said that his wife used enough paint on her face to paint a ship and enough powder to blow it up. The purpose of a mirror is to give an accurate reflection of the person looking into it.

James spoke of the auditor of God's word as being like a person who looked into the mirror and **beholdeth himself, and goeth his way, and straightway forgetteth what manner of man he was.** The word **beholdeth** carries the idea of a *"casual, haphazard glance."* He looks into the mirror and sees his face, but he goes on without concern. That is contrary to the purpose of mirrors. We look into the mirror to see what needs to be straightened out before we leave the house. The idea is to see what is wrong and then fix it.

But whoso looketh into the perfect law of liberty, and continueth therein, he being not a forgetful hearer, but a doer of the work, this man shall be blessed in his deed. (James 1:25) The word **looketh** means *"to bend beside, lean over, or to stoop down."* This is a strong word that carries the idea of applying one's self to observation. Notice James refers to the Bible as **the perfect law of liberty.** The idea is that those who follow the principles of the Word will experience true liberty. There will be freedom from slavery to sin. The Bible is a book of liberation. It is a book that when followed, sets men free from their sin to walk with and serves the living God of Glory.

And I will walk at liberty: for I seek thy precepts. (Psalms 119:45)

God's Word is a mirror that enables us to see ourselves as we are. James says that a **hearer** is like a person who takes a quick glance at the mirror and then immediately forgets what he saw. The **doer** looks intently into the mirror and does not forget. He sees what needs to be fixed and he fixes it. He doesn't plug his ears. He doesn't go shooting off his mouth.

He doesn't get mad at the preacher. He simply obeys the word of God. We need less auditing and more action.

REJECTION THAT CORRUPTS

A few verses later James says,. **If any man among you seem to be religious, and bridleth not his tongue, but deceiveth his own heart, this man's religion is vain. (James 1:26)** The word **religious** speaks of a profession of faith. He claims to be a God fearing man—a pious man. He attends Church, he sings hymns, maybe even puts a few dollars in the plate. He perceives himself as a good Christian.

But he **bridleth not his tongue.** The word bridle carries the idea of control. We use bridles on horses to control them. So here is a man who seems to be religious, but he cannot control his tongue. James says he, **deceiveth his own heart, this man's religion is vain.** The word vain means empty and worthless.

The illustrations of the bridle and the ships rudder used in chapter three shows how the tongue guides and controls the whole course of life. No wonder David said:

> ...I will take heed to my ways, that I sin not with my tongue: I will keep my mouth with a bridle, while the wicked is before me. (Psalms 39:1)

> **Whoso keepeth his mouth and his tongue keepeth his soul from troubles. (Proverbs 21:23)**

We can avoid a great deal of trouble by guarding our tongue. May God help us to keep our mouth bridled and under control.

Religion That Conquers

Pure religion and undefiled before God and the Father is this, To visit the fatherless and widows in their affliction, (James 1:27a) The man who gives the word of God free course in his life will be a changed man. The idea of the word **visit** is to *"oversee, to look after."* It is not a simple visit, it is an investment in them. Pure religion expresses itself in practical love for others. Pure religion reaches out to the lost, the least and the last.

> **Blessed is he that considereth the poor: the LORD will deliver him in time of trouble. (Psalms 41:1)**

> **A father of the fatherless, and a judge of the widows, is God in his holy habitation. (Psalms 68:5)**

There is something about helping the down-and-out that touches the heart of God.

James goes on to say, **and to keep himself unspotted from the world. (James 1:27b)** The idea behind **unspotted** is to be *"unstained."* He does not show evidence that he is worldly. He is pure as opposed to filthy. His separation from the world is seen in the purity of his ***Attitude***, ***Attire***, ***Associations***, ***Ambitions*** and the whole of his life.

Christians who compromise with the world and its ways, always end up spotted and stained by it's sin and wickedness. Sam P. Jones said:

> *If you lay down with the dogs, you will get up with fleas.*

The way to be unspotted is to be separated. Every Christians ought be separated from the world and unto God. Paul said:

> **Be not conformed to this world ... (Romans 12:2)**

> **Wherefore come out from among them, and be ye separate, saith the Lord, and touch not the unclean thing; and I will receive you, And will be a Father unto you, and ye shall be my sons and daughters, saith the Lord Almighty. (2 Corinthians 6:17-18)**

Everybody Is Somebody In God's House

James 2:1-13

James now deals with the problems of prejudice and partiality in the Church. For James to hit this matter as hard as he did there was no doubt a problem among the brethren of preferring some over others. Unfortunately this is a common problem.

The Dilemma Of Partiality

My brethren, have not the faith of our Lord Jesus Christ, the Lord of glory, with respect of persons. (James 2:1) We wouldn't think that there would be prejudice in the Church but there is. Paul said:

> **There is neither Jew nor Greek, there is neither bond nor free, there is neither male nor female: for ye are all one in Christ Jesus. (Galatians 3:28)**

In Christ is the one place that everyone truly is equal and that equality ought to be reflected in the Church.

The Problem Declared

Notice that James compares **the faith of our Lord Jesus Christ** with **respect of persons.** The point James is making is that true faith in the Lord Jesus Christ and prejudice can't go together. God loves and saves whosoever will come to Him. He does so without prejudice or partiality.

> **For the LORD your God is God of gods, and Lord of lords, a great God, a mighty, and a terrible, which regardeth not persons, nor taketh reward: (Deuteronomy 10:17)**

That God is not respecter of persons is clear from Scripture.

> **For there is no respect of persons with God. (Romans 2:11)**

> **Then Peter opened his mouth, and said, Of a truth I perceive that God is no respecter of persons: (Acts 10:34)**

> **And, ye masters, do the same things unto them, forbearing threatening: knowing that your Master also is in**

> heaven; neither is there respect of persons with him. (Ephesians 6:9)

Jesus Christ died for and loves everyone the same. The idea that James is trying to get across here is that it is inconsistent to say that we are saved by faith in Jesus Christ and at the same time be prejudice toward someone. We can't play favorites in the church on the one hand and, on the other, claim to have genuine faith in Jesus Christ.

THE PERSON DESCRIBED

James describes Jesus as **the Lord of glory. (James 2:1b)** This reminds us of the Shekinah glory of God. The word Shekinah means *"that which dwells."* In the Old Testament the word Shekinah spoke of God's glorious dwelling with man. When Solomon's Temple was dedicated God came in His Shekinah.

> **So that the priests could not stand to minister because of the cloud: for the glory of the LORD had filled the house of the LORD. (1 Kings 8:11)**

James describes **our Lord Jesus Christ** as the Shekinah glory of God. The point is that in the presence of Christ we are all insignificant. Therefore, who are we to look down our noses at someone else. In the radiance of Christ's glory all distinctions including monetary value, social standing and color disappear. The only one to get glory in the Christian's life is Jesus

Christ. When we focus on His glory we don't see the successes and failures or the prosperity and poverty of others—we see only Christ. He is the only One Who is worthy of glory.

THE PREJUDICE DEFINED

James describes partiality as **respect of persons. (James 2:1c)** The phrase **respect of persons** comes from two words that means *"to receive the face."* The idea is to show favor to a person based on what you see. To *"receive the face"* is to make judgments about someone based on external appearances such as physical looks, social status, or race. Jesus Christ is our supreme example. He never received or rejected anyone because of their color, social standing, or dress. Even the Pharisees and Herodians had to admit that Jesus treated everyone equal.

> **And they sent out unto him their disciples with the Herodians, saying, Master, we know that thou art true, and teachest the way of God in truth, neither carest thou for any man: for thou regardest not the person of men. (Matthew 22:16)**

It is unfortunate, but often God's people can fall into the pit of partiality. Often folks are partial based on:

Color —Partiality because of the color of one's skin.

Class—Partiality based on social standing.

Creed— Partiality based on religion.

Cash— Partiality based on one's financial status.

Such partiality and prejudice has no place in God's house. Prejudice is a work of the flesh. The new man has a renewed knowledge in this matter.

> **And have put on the new man, which is renewed in knowledge after the image of him that created him: Where there is neither Greek nor Jew, circumcision nor uncircumcision, Barbarian, Scythian, bond nor free: but Christ is all, and in all. (Colossians 3:10-11)**

The new man, that is the Spirit-filled man does not allow color, class, cash, or creed hinder him from reaching out to someone.

THE DEMONSTRATION OF PARTIALITY

> **For if there come unto your assembly a man with a gold ring, in goodly apparel, and there come in also a poor man in vile raiment; And ye have respect to him that weareth the gay clothing, and say unto him, Sit thou here in a good place; and say to the poor, Stand thou there, or sit here under my footstool: Are ye not then partial in yourselves, and**

are become judges of evil thoughts? (James 2:2-4) James gives an illustration of how prejudice works. Two visitors show up for church. The first visitor is dressed extravagantly; his **gold ring** is shining, his clothes are **goodly** and **gay**, meaning that his clothes are bright and magnificent. This guy is decked out. He is sharp. You can tell by the way he is dressed that he has money. The second visitor a **poor man in vile raiment.** The word **vile** means *"filthy."* This poor follow not only had no decent clothes, he didn't even have clean clothes. The church catered to the rich man and gave him the best seat in house, while neglecting the poor man. In his book, "Temptations Men Face," Tom Eisenman tells about an event that took place at Bel Aire Presbyterian Church:

> *"When in attendance, Governor Ronald Reagan and Nancy usually sat in the same seats just off the center aisle about two-thirds of the way into the sanctuary. On this particular morning the governor and his wife were late and by the time they got there, two college students had occupied those seats. An usher came down the aisle and asked the students if they would take different seats off to the side. They moved, and Ron and Nancy Reagan were brought in and seated. To his credit the pastor got up from his place in the chancel, walked down and over to the*

college students and said, "As long as I am pastor of this church, that will never happen to you again."

The Jews were big on fancy clothes and the best seats in the synagogue. Jesus said:

Beware of the scribes, which love to go in long clothing, and love salutations in the marketplaces, And the chief seats in the synagogues, and the uppermost rooms at feasts: (Mark 12:38-39)

They focused on the externals and neglected the heart and soul. This is what we are doing when we prefer someone over the other based on their appearance or social class. It is not a sin to be rich—to have expensive rings and clothes. Nor is it a sin to be poor. But it is sin to be prejudiced!

THE DISCREPANCY OF PARTIALITY

Hearken, my beloved brethren, Hath not God chosen the poor of this world rich in faith, and heirs of the kingdom which he hath promised to them that love him? (James 2:5) The word **hearken** is a call to listen attentively and emphasizes the importance of the instruction that is to follow. Once he has their attention, James issues an appeal for his readers to look at it from God's point of view. **Hath not God chosen the poor of this world rich in faith,**

and heirs of the kingdom which he hath promised to them that love him? God has a special place in His heart for the poor. The poor are often seen as insignificant in this world, but not in the Kingdom of God.

> **Blessed is he that considereth the poor: the LORD will deliver him in time of trouble. (Psalms 41:1)**
>
> **Thy congregation hath dwelt therein: thou, O God, hast prepared of thy goodness for the poor. (Psalms 68:10)**
>
> **He raiseth up the poor out of the dust, and lifteth the needy out of the dunghill; (Psalms 113:7)**
>
> **He shall judge the poor of the people, he shall save the children of the needy, and shall break in pieces the oppressor. (Psalms 72:4)**
>
> **For he shall deliver the needy when he crieth; the poor also, and him that hath no helper. (Psalms 72:12)**
>
> **Whoso mocketh the poor reproacheth his Maker: and he that is glad at calamities shall not be unpunished. (Proverbs 17:5)**

> **Whoso stoppeth his ears at the cry of the poor, he also shall cry himself, but shall not be heard. (Proverbs 21:13)**
>
> **He that giveth unto the poor shall not lack: but he that hideth his eyes shall have many a curse. (Proverbs 28:27)**
>
> **Open thy mouth, judge righteously, and plead the cause of the poor and needy. (Proverbs 31:9)**

We would do well to adapt God's thinking in this matter of partiality. God does not discriminate on the basis of money, skin color, or social standing. James refers to the poor as **chosen** and **heirs of the kingdom**. God honors the poor and if we dishonour them we dishonour God and His plan for them. **He that oppresseth the poor reproacheth his Maker ... (Proverbs 14:31)** The poor are so only in the world's estimation, not in God's.

But ye have despised the poor. Do not rich men oppress you, and draw you before the judgment seats? (James 2:6) The word **oppress** carries the idea of *"exercising power over"* over someone. Renn says that the word has the *"underlying sense of being harassed or tormented."* The word **draw** has the idea of *"forcefully dragging"* someone against their will.

Do not they blaspheme that worthy name by the which ye are called? (James 2:7) The **worthy name**

is the name of Christ. James says, **by the which ye are called.** When we call our self a Christian we identify with Christ. James pointed out that some of the big shots they were exalted in their services, were in fact blasphemers. James' argument is clear. Aren't the very ones you are exalting those who drag you to court and sue you and forcefully take your money. And on top of that they blaspheme the precocious name of Christ.

THE DEBAUCHERY OF PARTIALITY

If ye fulfil the royal law according to the scripture, Thou shalt love thy neighbour as thyself, ye do well: (James 2:8) This law of love is to influence the Christian's treatment of all men. This should especially be evident in the Church. Jesus dealt with the supreme importance of love when He answered the Pharisee's question concerning the greatest law.

> **But when the Pharisees had heard that he had put the Sadducees to silence, they were gathered together. Then one of them, which was a lawyer, asked him a question, tempting him, and saying, Master, which is the great commandment in the law? Jesus said unto him, Thou shalt love the Lord thy God with all thy heart, and with all thy soul, and with all thy mind. This is the**

first and great commandment. And the second is like unto it, Thou shalt love thy neighbour as thyself. On these two commandments hang all the law and the prophets. (Matthew 22:34-40)

James says that to be prejudice and show partiality is to violate the royal law of love. The word **law** speaks of that which is authoritative, absolute and binding—it is the authority by which we are governed. The word **royal** carries the ideas of supreme and sovereign and identifies this law as originating with and belonging to a king. When a sovereign king issues an decree, it is incontestably binding on all his subjects. There is no negotiation and no court of appeal.

But if ye have respect to persons, ye commit sin, and are convinced of the law as transgressors. For whosoever shall keep the whole law, and yet offend in one point, he is guilty of all. For he that said, Do not commit adultery, said also, Do not kill. Now if thou commit no adultery, yet if thou kill, thou art become a transgressor of the law. (James 2:9-11) When we are prejudice and show partiality we violate the royal law. Man has the tendency to classify his sin. They put sin into different categories and as long as they don't commit the sins in certain categories they feel pretty good about themselves. We hear about *"white lies"* and *"black lies."* We hear about *"little sins"* and *"big sins."* I heard a man say once, "Well I *might be a little prejudice, but I've never killed anyone and I'm not a thief."* James cuts these guys off at the pass. **For whosoever shall keep the whole law, and yet offend in one point, he is guilty of all. (James 2:10)** You can't be prejudice and claim to be a good Christian. James argues that though you may not have committed adultery, stole or killed anyone, you are nevertheless, **guilty of all.**

THE DEFEAT OF PARTIALITY

So speak ye, and so do, as they that shall be judged by the law of liberty. (James 2:12) James makes it clear that a day of judgment is coming. When Christ judges nothing will be hidden from Him.

> **All things are naked and opened unto the eyes of Him with whom they have to do. (Hebrews 4:13)**

Nothing can be hid from Him—He knows everything about us—even the secret things.

> **For God shall bring every work into judgment, with every secret thing, whether it be good, or whether it be evil. (Ecclesiastes 12:14)**

Nothing, not even the smallest detail, will escape His scrutiny.

> For the ways of man are before the eyes of the LORD, and he pondereth all his goings. (Proverbs 5:21)

God knows everything about you, every detail, every experience, every thought, every word, every work, every secret. If we have unconfessed and unforsaken sin in our life, the very thought of such a judgment ought to cause us to tremble.

… judged by the law of liberty. (James 2:12) The Word of God will be the basis or law at our judgment. Jesus said:

> ∂, … the word that I have spoken, the same shall judge him in the last day. (John 12:48)

We usually don't think terms of the **law of liberty**. Law contains liberty. However, the believer's liberty come from following the word of God.

> And I will walk at liberty: for I seek thy precepts. (Psalm 119:45)

For he shall have judgment without mercy, that hath shewed no mercy; and mercy rejoiceth against judgment. (James 2:13) God will show no mercy to the person who refuses to show mercy to others. Those who show no mercy will reap what they sow. If you go through life falsely judging people and having no mercy on them, that is exactly how you will stand before God. However, James says, **mercy rejoiceth against judgment**. Lehman Strauss wrote:

> *This means that mercy triumphs over judgment. If I show mercy to the needy instead of sitting in judgment upon them, I shall triumph in the end at the Judgment Seat of Christ. The Apostle John says that love has boldness in the day of judgment (1 John 4:17). Outward actions show very clearly what a man is at heart now, as well as what his reward will be hereafter. When a Christian shows compassion on others at all times, he looks forward to the judgment with calm confidence. A heart full of mercy has no fear of the day of judgment but rejoices in the face of it.*

In the day of God's judgment He will take into account how we judged others. Were our judgments of others merciful or unmerciful? **Blessed are the merciful: for they shall obtain mercy. (Matthew 5:7)** He will judge us the same way we judged others. **Herein is our love made perfect, that we may have boldness in the day of judgment: because as he is, so are we in this world. (1 John 4:17)**

Faith That Works

James 2:14-26

In this section James deals with the truth that genuine faith is an active faith. He is clear that a person who "talks the talk" must also "walk the walk." Empty lip service is not acceptable. The true believer lives what he believes. James declares that works is the outward demonstration that something real has happened in the heart. A person cannot be saved without a change taking place in his life. It may be slow, but it will be sure! Jesus, in the parable of the sower, taught this truth.

> **But he that received seed into the good ground is he that heareth the word, and understandeth it; which also beareth fruit, and bringeth forth, some an hundredfold, some sixty, some thirty. (Matthew 13:23)**

Every believer has the responsibility to live a biblical lifestyle. When a person gets saved, there will be fruit, ... **some an hundredfold, some sixty, some thirty.** Notice it does not say *"some zero,"* or *"some not any."* God's people—all of God's people are to be fruit bearers.

THE EMPTINESS OF DEAD FAITH

James deals first with the emptiness of dead faith pointing out that nothing of value is accomplished by such a faith.

DEAD FAITH IS VOCAL

What doth it profit, my brethren, though a man say he hath faith, and have not works? can faith save him? (James 2:14) In this section James contrasts the lip with the life. James makes it clear that it is useless to declare our faith when there is no demonstration of that faith. James says, **though a man say he hath faith.** Notice that James is talking about what a man says. Spitting out words is not a problem. Most folks talk far more than they should. Solomon said:

> **Most men will proclaim every one his own goodness: but a faithful man who can find? (Proverbs 20:6)**

We see this all the time—a pile of talk, but no faithfulness in the walk and work of God. James asks if he **have not works? can faith save him?** The idea here is that since there is no works as evidence of salvation, *"did faith save him?"* James questions whether such an individual is truly saved. God's people have a desire to serve Him.

Dead Faith Is Vain

If a brother or sister be naked, and destitute of daily food, And one of you say unto them, Depart in peace, be ye warmed and filled; notwithstanding ye give them not those things which are needful to the body; what doth it profit? (James 2:15-16) This faith is empty and accomplishes nothing of eternal value. James presents an illustration of someone who is without food and clothing. Notice the response of dead faith. **Depart in peace, be ye warmed and filled.** These are good words, but they do nothing to ease the pains of hunger, nor the bite of cold. James asks **what doth it profit?** The word **profit** carries the idea of *"gain, advantage, profit, accumulation."* There is no profit in mere talk. Our talk needs to be backed up by our walk. Too many people talk it by the mile but don't live it by the inch. Talk is cheap, but real faith manifests itself in action.

Dead Faith Is Void

Even so faith, if it hath not works, is dead, being alone. (James 2:17) Someone has well said *"Faith alone saves, but faith that saves is not alone."* We live in a day of empty professions. A day when folks talk about repeating a prayer, but they produce no evidence of salvation. John the Baptist would not have considered them saved. He certainly wouldn't have baptized them. He believed that folks ought to demonstrate a changed life. The Pharisees and Sadducees were extremely vocal about their religion, but when they came to John for baptism he said:

> **Bring forth therefore fruits meet for repentance: (Matthew 3:8)**

The word **meet** comes from *"axios"* and refers to a set of balances or scales. The word means, *"having the weight of another thing of like value, worth as much."* The idea is that if one is saved, his life will balance out with his profession.

James says, **Yea, a man may say, Thou hast faith, and I have works: shew me thy faith without thy works, and I will shew thee my faith by my works. (James 2:18)** Genuine faith is seen in our work for God. Jesus said:

> **Let your light so shine before men, that they may see your good works, and glorify your Father which is in heaven. (Matthew 5:16)**

Salvation changes things. Life is no longer life as usual. While salvation is apart from works, it is certainly unto works. Paul preached the same doctrine.

> For we are his workmanship, created in Christ Jesus unto good works, which God hath before ordained that we should walk in them. (Ephesians 2:10)
>
> That being justified by his grace, we should be made heirs according to the hope of eternal life. This is a faithful saying, and these things I will that thou affirm constantly, that they which have believed in God might be careful to maintain good works. These things are good and profitable unto men. (Titus 3:7-8) Just a little earlier the Bible said that He gave himself for us, that he might redeem us from all iniquity, and purify unto himself a peculiar people, zealous of good works. (Titus 2:14)

God's purpose in saving us goes beyond simply rescuing us from Hell. We are saved to serve.

THE EVIDENCE OF DEMONIC FAITH

> Thou believest that there is one God; thou doest well: the devils also believe, and tremble. (James 2:19)

A mere intellectual belief is not enough to be saved; there must be a heart belief. The Christian life is lived from the heart, not from the head. James makes it clear that just to believe in God is not sufficient to be called a saving faith, for even the Devil and his demons believe in God. James points out that the **devils also believe, and tremble.** The Devil and his demons are well aware of who God is and the fact that He is their Judge. When two demon-possessed men met Jesus, the Bible says the demons:

> **... cried out, saying, What have we to do with thee, Jesus, thou Son of God? art thou come hither to torment us before the time? (Matthew 8:29)**

These demons believed in God and His coming judgment. Their faith moved them to fear Jesus Christ. Another incident is recorded in Mark.

> **And there was in their synagogue a man with an unclean spirit; and he cried out, Saying, Let us alone; what have we to do with thee, thou Jesus of Nazareth? art thou come to destroy us? I know thee who thou art, the Holy One of God. (Mark 1:23-24)**

The point is that even the demons believe in God, but it doesn't save them. If you ask Satan, "Do you believe that Jesus is God?" He would say, "yes." If he was asked "Do you believe in the virgin birth?," he would say "yes." If he was asked "Do you believe the bible is God's word?," he would say, "yes." Satan has the theology, but the theology doesn't have him.

James adds **But wilt thou know, O vain man, that faith without works is dead? (James 2:20)** A man who's faith produces no fruit is call a **vain man**. The word **vain** means *"empty, shallow."* James is saying, *"you empty and shallow man."* It is an empty and shallow faith that claims to know God, but does not manifest itself in service to God. A faith that does not produce fruit is useless. Dead faith moves only the lips, it doesn't affect the life.

The Energy Of Dynamic Faith

To illustrate the great truth of dynamic faith James draws on two Old Testament people that his Jewish readers would be familiar with. It is important to point out here that the people of the Old Testament were saved the same way as the people of the New Testament—that is by faith. The Bible is clear those who lived under the law were not saved by keeping the law.

> **Knowing that a man is not justified by the works of the law, but by the faith of Jesus Christ, even we have believed in Jesus Christ, that we might be justified by the faith of Christ, and not by the works of the law: for by the works of the law shall no flesh be justified. (Galatians 2:16)**

In the Old Testament God's people looked forward to the coming of Christ in faith while New Testament believers look back to the cross of Christ in faith. James uses these illustrations to point out how faith is demonstrated or proven by works.

The Patriarch—Abraham

Was not Abraham our father justified by works, when he had offered Isaac his son upon the altar? (James 2:21) Now Paul said, **For if Abraham were justified by works, he hath whereof to glory; but not before God. (Romans 4:2)** At first glance, Paul and James seem to contradict each other on this point. Martin Luther stumbled at these verses and called James a *"straw epistle,"* even suggesting that the book wasn't inspired and shouldn't be included in the cannon of Scripture. Such an explanation is not an option. The Bible is the one perfect book! When something doesn't seem to fit the problem is not with God's word, it is with our limited minds. Now notice how this is cleared up.

First, the **<u>Declaration of Abraham's Faith</u>**. **And the scripture was fulfilled which saith, Abraham believed God, and it was imputed unto him for righteousness: and he was called the Friend of God. (James 2:23)** James is quoting from the book of Genesis where the first mention of Abraham's being declared righteous is found.

> And he believed in the LORD; and he counted it to him for righteousness. (Genesis 15:6)

Notice the reason Abraham was declared righteous —**he believed God.** This statement is in perfect harmony with Paul's writing.

> For what saith the scripture? Abraham believed God, and it was counted unto him for righteousness. (Romans 4:3)

In Galatians Paul makes the same point.

> Even as Abraham believed God, and it was accounted to him for righteousness. (Galatians 3:6)

It is for certain that Abraham was saved by faith alone with no mixture of works. The Bible is in perfect harmony on this matter of salvation by faith alone. The fact that James quotes Genesis 15:6 shows he believes and understands this truth of justification by faith alone. Then what exactly did James mean when he speaks of Abraham being justified by works? That brings us to …

Second, the **<u>Demonstration of Abraham's Faith</u>**. **Was not Abraham our father justified by works, when he had offered Isaac his son upon the altar? (James 2:21)** Notice that James is taking about a specific time in Abraham's life when he **offered Isaac**

his son upon the altar. As we have already seen Abraham's justification by God took place in Genesis 15:6. However, James' illustration is drawn from the offering of Isaac, an event that took place some 40 years later. The sacrifice of Isaac was a great act faith.

> **By faith Abraham, when he was tried, offered up Isaac: and he that had received the promises offered up his only begotten son, (Hebrews 11:17)**

James is not talking about how Abraham was saved, but how his faith is seen in his faithfulness to God. Our faith is made visible by our faithfulness. Our obedience proves to others that our faith in God is genuine. Paul spoke concerning how Abraham became justified **before God (Romans 4:2)**, and James spoke of how Abraham was justified before his fellowman by giving evidence of having true faith. That is why James used expressions such as **seest thou... (James 2:22)** and **ye see then. (2:24)** The point James is making is that saving faith is working faith. Forty years after his salvation experience, Abraham's faith is still working.

THE PROSTITUTE—RAHAB

Likewise also was not Rahab the harlot justified by works, when she had received the messengers, and had sent them out another way? For as the body without the spirit is dead, so faith without works is dead also. (James 2:25-26) Rahab is another example of someone who lived by dynamic faith rather than dead faith. Rahab stands in stark contrast to Abraham. Abraham was the faithful hero of God's chosen people, Rahab was the foreign harlot of a pagan people. They come from different ends of the spectrum, but they were saved the same way—by faith.

> **For by grace are ye saved through faith; and that not of yourselves: it is the gift of God: Not of works, lest any man should boast. (Ephesians 2:8-9)**

The historical account of Rahab is recorded in Joshua chapter two. She gave her testimony clearly:

> **...the LORD your God, he is God in heaven above, and in earth beneath. (Joshua 2:11)**

Rahab serves a wonderful example of working faith. She is mentioned in the Faith's Hall Of Fame.

> **By faith the harlot Rahab perished not with them that believed not, when she had received the spies with peace. (Hebrews 11:31)**

Rahab believed that the one and only God of Heaven was going to give the land of Canaan to the people of Israel. She demonstrated her faith by hiding the spies and sending their pursuers off in another direction. Later, she helped the spies to escape. If the rulers of

Jericho had known of her disloyalty, they would have put her to death. But that didn't matter as much to Rahab as her loyalty to God. Rahab's faith in Israel's God caused her to protect His people. Rahab's faith was declared in Joshua 2:11 when she said:

> **...the LORD your God, he is God in heaven above, and in earth beneath. (Joshua 2:11)**

But her faith was demonstrated in Joshua 2:21 when she saved the spies and sent them out another way. Joshua six records the fall of the walls and the conquering of Jericho. But it also records how Rahab and her household was spared. The point James is making is that Rahab's faith was seen by what she did.

Don't Get Hung By Your Tongue

James 3:1-12

Sins of the tongue were very common in the time of James; in fact they always have been, and are so today. I agree with Dr. John R. Rice who said, *"More people sin with the tongue than any other way."* An unbridled tongue has caused much trouble and turmoil in the world, and unfortunately among Christians as well.

The Product Of The Tongue

James says, **My brethren, be not many masters ... (James 3:1a)** The word **masters** here is an old English word that simply means *"teachers."* In Jewish culture teachers were held in great admiration. In the Old Testament, teachers were called *"Rabbis."* The word itself means *"great one."* Being a teacher of God's Word involves the instructing and directing of other people's lives. Therefore, such a work is a solemn responsibility. James urges that believers, especially those young in the faith, not be overzealous or over anxious to impart their knowledge. They need first of all to study, learn, and grow in spiritual matters.

James says, ... **knowing that we shall receive the greater condemnation. (James 3:1b)** The word **condemnation** comes from the Greek word *"krima"* and it means *"judgment."* Preaching and teaching the Word of God is one of the greatest privileges that God gives to man. However, because it is a ministry that affects the lives of others in such a great way, God will judge the teacher with more scrutiny. In other words the judgment of God will be more severe for the teacher. With privilege comes responsibility and responsibility brings accountability. The Lord will hold us responsible for those we teach. Jesus taught the same thing.

> **And he said unto them in his doctrine, Beware of the scribes, which love to go in long clothing, and love salutations in the marketplaces, And the chief seats in the synagogues, and the uppermost rooms at feasts: Which devour widows' houses, and for a pretence make long prayers: these shall receive greater damnation. (Mark 12:38-40)**

The Preacher and the teacher are to use their tongues to **Enlighten**, **Establish**, **Exhort**, **Encourage**, and **Edify** others. What a serious undertaking it is to teach others. If one fails in this matter of teaching and declaring the whole counsel of God's Word, God will hold him accountable for misleading his hearers, whether done through ignorance of the Word or through neglect. Paul was able to say:

> **Wherefore I take you to record this day, that I am pure from the blood of all men. For I have not shunned to declare unto you all the counsel of God. (Acts 20:26-27)**

Had Paul been careless and negligent in proclaiming and explaining God's Word he would have been guilty of the hearer's blood. James says those responsible for proclaiming the Word will **receive the greater condemnation.**

For in many things we offend all ... (James 3:2a) The word offend means *"to fail, stumble or to err."* The truth of the matter is that no one is exempt in regard to the dangers of the tongue. No one is perfect and that adds even more weight to James' warning.

James goes on to say, **If any man offend not in word, the same is a perfect man, and able also to bridle the whole body. (James 3:2b)** The word **bridle** in verse two means to control or restrain.

James uses this illustration to help us understand how the tongue guides and controls the whole course of life. Douglas Moo said:

> *So difficult is the mouth to control, so given is it to utter the false, the biting, the slanderous word, so prone to stay open when it were more profitably closed, that the person who has it in control surely has the ability to conquer other, less unruly, members of the body.*

No wonder David said:

> **I said, I will take heed to my ways, that I sin not with my tongue: I will keep my mouth with a bridle, while the wicked is before me. (Psalms 39:1)**

A persons tongue can quickly get hime into more trouble than he get out of.

THE POWER OF THE TONGUE

Behold, we put bits in the horses' mouths, that they may obey us; and we turn about their whole body. (James 3:3) A bit in a horse's mouth is such a small thing but just think of the service it delivers. James says that we use these bits in horses' mouths **that they may obey us.** A.B. Simpson wrote:

> *Just as a man's mouth is the test of his character, so the horse's mouth is the*

place to control him. We put bits in their mouths, and by these turn about their whole body, so that a little bit of steel and a little thong of leather will hold a fiery steed, and turn him at the touch of a woman's hand. So the tongue is like a bridle, which can be put upon us. With a fiery horse you put a curb in his bit The idea is to hurt him, if he pulls against the bit So God has given to us checks upon our tongue, making it hurt us, if we speak unadvisedly.

A horse is a powerful creature with a mind of its own. Left to itself the horse goes where it wants to. But by inserting a small bit in the horse's mouth a rider can control the direction of the horse. The bit is indeed a little thing, but it controls the horse.

Behold also the ships, which though they be so great, and are driven of fierce winds, yet are they turned about with a very small helm, whithersoever the governor listeth. (James 3:4) The second illustration is that of a ship being driven every which way by the fierce winds. By simply moving a very **small helm** a huge ship can be **turned ... whithersoever the governor listeth.** With just a slight turn of the wrist the small rudder moves and the Captain guides the vessel where he wants it to go in spite of the strong winds.

A little bit controlled the direction of the horse. A little rudder controlled the direction of the ship. Notice in both cases something small controlled the direction of something that was much bigger. James' illustrations are meant to teach us that our tongue controls the direction of our life.

THE PERIL OF THE TONGUE

Even so the tongue is a little member, and boasteth great things... (James 3:5a) Like the bit and the rudder **the tongue is a little member. (James 3:5)**, but it guides with great influence. Though the tongue is little, it **boasteth great things.** Solomon said:

> **Death and life are in the power of the tongue ... (Proverbs 18:21)**

Although the tongue is small, it exercises immense power, and it can make or break a person's life or testimony and do great damage to others as well.

THE TONGUE IS A FIRE

Behold, how great a matter a little fire kindleth! And the tongue is a fire, a world of iniquity: so is the tongue among our members, that it defileth the whole body, and setteth on fire the course of nature; and it is set on fire of hell. (James 3:5b-6) By comparing it to a fire, James points out that the tongue has tremendous power to destroy. All it takes is a single spark to do great damage. Many forest fires have been started by the tiny spark of one match or cigarette carelessly thrown away. Just a tiny spark from a dying campfire has resulted in destroying thousands of acres of timber not to mention the wildlife destroyed. Many lives have been taken and many homes and businesses destroyed because of fire. A little fire and a little word are a lot alike, both can do enormous damage. What power just one word can have. Just like one little seemingly insignificant spark, at first it seems to be nothing, but it soon destroys everything in its path. Nothing good comes from a loose and uncontrolled tongue. Solomon said,:

> **... the mouth of the wicked poureth out evil things. (Proverbs 15:28)**

David said:

> **My soul is among lions: and I lie even among them that are set on fire, even the sons of men, whose teeth are spears and arrows, and their tongue a sharp sword. (Psalms 57:4)**

In his book, "Faith That Works," George Sweeting quotes Morgan Blake, a sportswriter for the Atlanta Journal who wrote:

> "I am more deadly than the screaming shell from the howitzer. I win without killing. I tear down homes, break hearts,

and wreck lives. I travel on the wings of the wind. No innocence is strong enough to intimidate me, no purity pure enough to daunt me. I have no regard for truth, no respect for justice, no mercy for the defenseless. My victims are as numerous as the sands of the sea, and often as innocent. I never forget and seldom forgive. My name is Gossip."

James tells us that the smoldering tongue is not lit with any ordinary fire, it is **set on fire of hell.** The work of the uncontrolled tongue is a product of hell. A person who cannot control his or her tongue is doing the Devil's work. **Contentious**, **Critical**, and **Careless** tongues have caused untold damage and hindered God's work over and over. James warned earlier that:

> **If any man among you seem to be religious, and bridleth not his tongue, but deceiveth his own heart, this man's religion is vain. (James 1:26)**

One who claims to be a Christian, but can't control his mouth is deceived and his religion is empty and worthless. Solomon said:

> **An ungodly man diggeth up evil: and in his lips there is as a burning fire. (Proverbs 16:27)**

Anyone who is constantly talking about and tearing away at others has a deceived heart, his religion is vain and he is not God's man. Solomon said:

THE TONGUE IS FIERCE

For every kind of beasts, and of birds, and of serpents, and of things in the sea, is tamed, and hath been tamed of mankind: (James 3:7) While man can tame the meanest and deadliest of wild beasts he can't tame his own tongue. Just think of the wild animals that pounce, prowl and kill and yet can be tamed! **But the tongue can no man tame ... (James 3:8a)** Notice James didn't say the tongue couldn't be tamed, but that **no man** can tame the tongue. We need God's help with the tongue. **Set a watch, O LORD, before my mouth; keep the door of my lips. (Psalms 141:3)**

THE TONGUE IS FATAL

The tongue is described as **an unruly evil, full of deadly poison. (James 3:8b)** Like the poison of a viper, the tongue is armed with the lethal venom of hate, hostility, and destructive, deadly gossip. We say "talk is cheap," but the fact of the matter is, no amount of money can buy back what we say. Once it leaves our mouth it is out there. Solomon said:

> An hypocrite with his mouth destroyeth his neighbor ... (Proverbs 11:9a)

Like the deadly poison of a viper, the tongue spews forth its venom in the form of gossip, slander, malice, anger and envy. The loose tongue can be the beginning of unbelievable strife, severed friendships, spilt churches, divorces, broken homes, and even wars.

THE PARADOX OF THE TONGUE

Therewith bless we God, even the Father; and therewith curse we men, which are made after the similitude of God. (James 3:9) The word **bless** means *"to speak well of, to praise."* To speak and sing praises unto our Great God and Saviour is the highest privilege known to man. The tongue has no greater task.

> Bless the LORD, O my soul: and all that is within me, bless his holy name. Bless the LORD, O my soul, and forget not all his benefits. (Psalms 103:1-2)

The word **curse** is the opposite of **bless**. It is a pronouncement of evil against someone. James says while they were busy blessing God, they were cursing man who were made after the similitude of God. In the Old testament the highest form of praise for someone was a blessing. A curse was just the opposite. It was the lowest form of speech. The tragedy is that with the same tongue with which we speak so highly of God, therewith curse we men, which are made after the similitude of God.

Out of the same mouth proceedeth blessing and cursing. My brethren, these things ought not so to be. (James 3:10) To praise God and then curse men who are made in the image of God is blatant hypocrisy. Our being made in the image of God is the reason for not cursing our fellow man. We are expressly forbidden to curse anyone.

Bless them which persecute you: bless, and curse not. (Romans 12:14)

Doth a fountain send forth at the same place sweet water and bitter? (James 3:11) Does the same fountain bring forth bitter and sweet water? The answer is evident, whatever kind of water that is in the well comes out of the faucet. Whether bad or good water that is what you get. The whole concept of getting two kinds of water out of the same well is contrary to nature. The same is true of the believer. Anyone who can sit in Church and praise God, then go forth spewing hatred and bitterness toward others has a serious problem.

James then asks the question, **Can the fig tree, my brethren, bear olive berries? either a vine, figs? (James 3:12)** Again, the answer is obvious! This too goes against the very laws of nature which were established by God.

> **And God said, Let the earth bring forth grass, the herb yielding seed, and the fruit tree yielding fruit after his kind, whose seed is in itself, upon the earth: and it was so. (Genesis 1:11)**

Everything produces after its own kind. Just as a fountain is known by the water it gives and a tree by its fruit, man's heart is known by what the tongue speaks. No wonder Harry Ironside called the tongue *"the index of the heart."*

The Importance Of Heavenly Wisdom

James 3:13-18

We live in the information age. Knowledge is exploding. There are more people graduating from Colleges and Universities than ever before. Textbooks and Encyclopedias are out of date almost as soon as they are printed. With the internet we have hordes of information at our fingertips with just a few clicks of the mouse. But in the midst of the knowledge, there is a serious lack of wisdom.

Wisdom is important. The word **wisdom** carries the idea of *"skillfulness.* "The idea is that of a workman having ability and skill at what he does. In Biblical context, wisdom is the God given ability to use knowledge properly. Noah Webster defines wisdom as:

> *"The right use or exercise of knowledge; the choice of laudable ends, and of the best means to accomplish them. This is*

wisdom in act, effect, or practice."

This word was used to describe the ability of the craftsmen who worked in the tabernacle.

And I, behold, I have given with him Aholiab, the son of Ahisamach, of the tribe of Dan: and in the hearts of all that are wise hearted I have put wisdom, that they may make all that I have commanded thee; (Exodus 31:6)

Wisdom is the skill or ability to practice what one knows. We must not mistake knowledge for wisdom! A person with a college degree may have a great deal of knowledge, but no common sense. However, wisdom is the ability to understand and to discern what to do, how to do it, and when to do it. In this section James points out that there are two kinds of wisdom. He contrasts the Wisdom of the World with the Wisdom of the Word.

The Proof Of Wisdom

Who is a wise man and endued with knowledge among you? let him shew out of a good conversation his works with meekness of wisdom. (James 3:13) James begins to deal with the relationship between wisdom and behavior. He doesn't mince words. He says in clear terms that if we talk it we are to walk it. David Sorenson says:

> *"The thought undoubtedly hearkens back to verse 1 of this chapter, referring to those who advanced themselves as (wise) teachers. If they so considered themselves such, James advised for them to first demonstrate through their lives whatever wisdom they claimed to possess."*

James speaks about being **wise** and **endued with knowledge. (James 3:13a)** These are two different things. There is a vast difference between wisdom and knowledge. There are a lot of folks that are endued with knowledge, but have little or no wisdom. Knowledge is the accumulation of information. Wisdom is the ability to take information and put it into action at the point of need. James gives us two characteristics of Godly Wisdom.

Holiness

James says if a man is wise and endued with knowledge ... **let him shew out of a good conversation his works ... (James 3:13b)** Wisdom is associated with holiness. Wisdom promotes purity in the believer's life. James says **let him shew.** The word **shew** means to *"expose or to demonstrate."* A wise person demonstrates his wisdom by **good conversation.** The word **conversation** carries the idea of *"behavior or conduct."* There are two kinds of conversation. *First*, there is that which we say with our

lips. *Secondly*, there it that which we say with our **_life_**. James is not speaking of our talk, but our walk—our manner of life. He is talking about how we live from day to day. We give evidence of our wisdom by good behavior. When the word of God takes root in one's life there will be a corresponding change in behavior.

HUMILITY

James goes on to say that such wisdom is demonstrated **with meekness of wisdom. (James 3:13c)** Now this is an interesting word. **Meekness** is a word that basically means *"mild," "gentle,"* or *"softness of temper."* Meekness is not weakness or a lack of power. Rather, it is power under control. This word was used for a horse that had been broken. The horse wasn't powerless, just broken. The horse was just as powerful as he ever was, but now he is under control and able to be turned in any direction by the will of its master. Jesus is the perfect example of meekness.

> **Take my yoke upon you, and learn of me; for I am meek and lowly in heart: and ye shall find rest unto your souls. (Matthew 11:29)**

Meekness has the strength to control and discipline one's self. It is a requirement for reaching people.

> **In meekness instructing those that oppose themselves; if God peradventure**

will give them repentance to the acknowledging of the truth. (2 Timothy 2:25)

It is a requirement for restoring the fallen.

Brethren, if a man be overtaken in a fault, ye which are spiritual, restore such an one in the spirit of meekness; considering thyself, lest thou also be tempted. (Galatians 6:1)

The wisdom of God produces meekness in our life as we are conformed to the image of Christ. As we become more like our Saviour we will display a greater meekness.

THE PERVERSION OF WISDOM

But if ye have bitter envying and strife in your hearts, glory not, and lie not against the truth. This wisdom descendeth not from above, but is earthly, sensual, devilish. For where envying and strife is, there is confusion and every evil work. (James 3:14-16) James now deals with perverted wisdom. Perverted wisdom is not from above. It is not God's wisdom. James says, **if ye have bitter envying and strife in your hearts, glory not, and lie not against the truth.** James is not referring so much to philosophical truth or scientific truth as he is the truth of the word of God. When we acquire God's wisdom it changes our life. On the other hand, to claim to have wisdom and yet live contrary to the word of God is to *"lie against the truth."* James identifies perverted worldly wisdom in three ways.

PERVERTED WISDOM IS SECULAR

This wisdom descendeth not from above, but is earthly... (James 3:15a) The word **earthly** means *"belonging to the earth."* It is secular as opposed to spiritual. It speaks of that which comes from this fallen world rather than **from above**. It indicates that which is wicked and sinful.

> **For many walk, of whom I have told you often, and now tell you even weeping, that they are the enemies of the cross of Christ: Whose end is destruction, whose God is their belly, and whose glory is in their shame, who mind earthly things. (Philippians 3:18-19)**

Earthly wisdom is practiced by those who have no grasp on heavenly wisdom. This is a wisdom that rather than embracing God's truth, it explains it away.

PERVERTED WISDOM IS SENSUAL

This wisdom descendeth not from above, but is sensual. (James 3:15b) Sensual wisdom is wisdom that seeks to accommodate our senses. Sensual comes from the word *"psychikos,"* which means *"the soul."* It is derived from *"psyche,"* the word from which we get *"psychology."* Man is a Trichotomy. He consists of three parts—body, soul and spirit. The body relates to self, the soul to the world, but spirit to God. James uses the word sensual speaking of the soul—the part of man that relates to the world. This has to do with the natural and the depraved. Paul said:

> **But the natural man receiveth not the things of the Spirit of God: for they are foolishness unto him: neither can he know them, because they are spiritually discerned. (1 Corinthians 2:14)**

Perverted wisdom is wisdom that is typical of human nature, not divine nature.

PERVERTED WISDOM IS SATANIC

This wisdom descendeth not from above, but is **devilish. (James 3:15c)** Satan is identified as the driving force behind the wisdom of this world. Perverted wisdom has its roots in Hell. It is tragic, but true, that the world and the Church are filled with satanic wisdom.

> **Now the Spirit speaketh expressly, that in the latter times some shall depart from the faith, giving heed to seducing spirits, and doctrines of devils; Speaking lies in hypocrisy;**

having their conscience seared with a hot iron; Forbidding to marry, and commanding to abstain from meats, which God hath created to be received with thanksgiving of them which believe and know the truth. For every creature of God is good, and nothing to be refused, if it be received with thanksgiving: For it is sanctified by the word of God and prayer. (1 Timothy 4:1-5)

For such are false apostles, deceitful workers, transforming themselves into the apostles of Christ. And no marvel; for Satan himself is transformed into an angel of light. Therefore it is no great thing if his ministers also be transformed as the ministers of righteousness; whose end shall be according to their works. (2 Corinthians 11:13-15)

Satan has his theology. It is cloaked in Church rhetoric, but it is dangerous and its origin is Hell. That's right! Many Churches have been infiltrated with the doctrines of Hell. Satan is smart and shrewd. He knows how to peddle his wickedness and error. He propagates his evil in Bible language and many Christians swallow it hook, line and sinker. Even with the temptation of Christ the devil was slick and sly. He was worldly wise in his approach. He even used Scripture. Actually he misused Scripture.

THE PRACTICE OF WISDOM

But the wisdom that is from above is first pure, then peaceable, gentle, and easy to be intreated, full of mercy and good fruits, without partiality, and without hypocrisy. (James 3:17) When we practice God's wisdom there are several characteristics that shows up in our life.

GOD'S WISDOM IS PURE

But the wisdom that is from above is first pure... (James 3:17a) Notice James says that this wisdom is **first pure**. Above all else, this wisdom is pure. The word **pure** carries the idea of *"being free of contamination or defilement."* It is the doctrine of holiness. God still commands His children.

> **Be ye holy; for I am holy. (1 Peter 1:16)**

God takes our holiness seriously.

> **Having therefore these promises, dearly beloved, let us cleanse ourselves from all filthiness of the flesh and spirit, perfecting holiness in the fear of God. (2 Corinthians 7:1)**

This is something that we are to be perfecting on our lives. The word **perfecting** carries the idea of *"finishing, completing, and fulfilling."* Peter wrote:

> **Seeing then that all these things shall be dissolved, what manner of persons ought ye to be in all holy conversation and godliness. (2 Peter 3:11)**

Purity is to be one of the dominate characteristics of the believer's life. Paul warned:

> **... neither be partaker of other men's sins: keep thyself pure. (1 Timothy 5:22)**

James connects our purity with biblical wisdom. If we are truly wise we will seek to be pure in our walk.

God's Wisdom Is Peaceable

True wisdom is **peaceable. (James 3:17b)** Real wisdom promotes peace. A few verses later James says, **And the fruit of righteousness is sown in peace of them that make peace. (James 3:18)** Jesus said:

> **Blessed are the peacemakers: for they shall be called the children of God. (Matthew 5:9)**

Some folks never seem to have peace. Turmoil follows them everywhere they go. They fight with family. They fight with friends. They fight with church.

They have trouble at work. They have no peace. They are not peacemakers, they are troublemakers!

> **But the wicked are like the troubled sea, when it cannot rest, whose waters cast up mire and dirt. There is no peace, saith my God, to the wicked. (Isaiah 57:20-21)**

The lost world does not know the peace of God.

> **There is no peace, saith the LORD, unto the wicked. (Isaiah 48:22)**

However, will there are some folks that we can't be at peace with, but it ought not to be our fault.

> **If it be possible, as much as lieth in you, live peaceably with all men. (Romans 12:18)**

> **Follow peace with all men, and holiness, without which no man shall see the Lord: (Hebrews 12:14)**

Peace comes from an unwavering trust in the Saviour. True and lasting peace is the fruit of a right relationship with God.

God's Wisdom Is Patient

True wisdom is **gentle. (James 3:17c)** The believer will face many trials in his life and God's wisdom teaches us to be patient in those trials. Trails are not intended to destroy us, but to build us. Gentleness is one of the characteristics of a successful servant. Paul said:

> **And the servant of the Lord must not strive; but be gentle unto all men, apt to teach, patient. (2 Timothy 2:24)**

The word **gentle** carries the idea of being *"yielding, unassertive,* or *lenient."* Renn in his *"Expository Dictionary of Bible Words"* says that it means *"'gentle' in relation to a kindly, patient disposition of spirit."* One writer says the following about the man who is gentle.

> *"He knows how to forgive when strict justice gives him a perfect right to condemn. He knows how to make allowances, when not to stand upon his rights, how to temper justice with mercy, always remembers that there are greater things in the world than rules and regulations."*

Gentleness is a fruit of the Spirit (Galatians 5:22). In essence, gentleness is grace in action. True wisdom will have compassion even when it has the right to condemn.

God's Wisdom Is Practical

True wisdom is **easy to be intreated. (James 3:17d)** This is an interesting word. It means *"to be* *reasonable about a matter."* A describes one who has a willingness to listen to reason and be practical and reasonable about the matter. Jesus was a good example. Anyone could come to Him at any time and He was ready to hear and help them. The lepers could come. Sinful women came to Him. Even a self-righteous Pharisee by the name of Nicodemus came to Him and found Him easy to be entreated.

GOD'S WISDOM IS PRODUCTIVE

True wisdom is **full of mercy and good fruits**. **(James 3:17e)** The word **mercy** carries the idea of *"having feelings of pity, compassion and kindness."* It carries the idea of having a desire to tenderly draw someone under your care and tend to their needs. James also mentions **good fruits.** Fruit is the result of showing mercy. Mercy opens the door for us help and influence others for Christ. People will respond more positively to mercy quicker than they will to criticism. God's wisdom motivates us to build up rather than tear down.

GOD'S WISDOM IS PRINCIPLED

True wisdom is **without partiality. (James 3:17f)** The wise person is impartial. His judgments are based on principle rather than personality. He shows no partiality or favoritism to anyone. The word is *"adiakritos"* and means *"unwavering."* It carries the idea of not being divided and vacillating back and forth. Wisdom does not treat one person a certain way and someone else another away. When God's wisdom is guiding our life we will be impartial.

GOD'S WISDOM IS PARTICULAR

True wisdom is **without hypocrisy. (James 3:17g)** Hypocrisy is the act of disguising oneself and hiding or operating under a false appearance. Noah Webster defines a hypocrite as:

> *"One who feigns to be what he is not; one who has the form of godliness without the power, or who assumes an appearance of piety and virtue, when he is destitute of true religion."*

The word hypocrite was originally a theatrical term. It was used in the Greek and Roman theaters to describe an actor. A lot of professing Christians fit the definition. Jesus dealt firmly with the hypocrites in (Matthew 23:1-13), who were wicked men pretending to be holy and righteous. They were leading people to hell by just putting on an act of religion. There is no place for such a lifestyle and wisdom rejects it.

Worldly Conflict In God's House

James 4:1-12

The one place on earth where there ought to be harmony is in the Church. God's house should be known as place of peace and unity. God desires that His people enjoy unity.

> **Behold, how good and how pleasant it is for brethren to dwell together in unity! (Psalms 133:1)**

Unity among believers pleases the Lord. However, many Churches are engulfed in conflict. From the earliest days Churches have had to deal with internal strife. The problem is the flesh and all that comes along with it—pride, selfishness, envy, gossip and a host of other sins.

We remember that the members of the Corinthian church were suffering discord because of their carnality. There were similar problems in the Galatian Church. Paul warned them:

> **But if ye bite and devour one another, take heed that ye be not consumed one of another. (Galatians 5:15)**

James points out the causes and cure for conflict in the Church.

The Cause Of Conflict

From whence come wars and fightings among you? come they not hence, even of your lusts that war in your members? (James 4:1) James starts by identifying the Source and the Symptoms of conflict in the Church.

The Symptoms Of Conflict

The word **wars (James 4:1a)** speaks of *"a long-drawn-out resentment."* It is not speaking of a quick battle that erupts and is over in a little while. It is more of a long drawn out war. The word **fightings** speaks of *"strife," "contention,"* or *"quarreling."* There are many believers who live this way. They are always at war with someone—wrangling and squabbling and fussing. You would think that their calling in life is to cause trouble. You start sowing discord and strife and you will become an enemy of God in a hurry. God has made it clear that He hates one **that soweth discord among brethren. (Proverbs 6:19b)**

THE SOURCE OF CONFLICT

James answers the question he just asked, **come they not hence, even of your lusts that war in your members? (James 4:1b)** The word translated **lusts** speaks of *"sensual pleasure."* It comes from the word *"hedone,"* from which the word *"hedonism"* is derived. It speaks of the practice of living for the satisfying of sensual desires. The New Testament always uses this word in the sinful sense. Hedonism is the bane of our day. We live in a pleasure drunk society. The philosophy of the day is *"if it feels good, do it!"*

James identified the source as the **lusts that war in your members. (James 4:1c)** Where does it come from? It comes from within. The word **members** refers to the physical and mental elements of the body—that which contains man's flesh. The flesh speaks of what a man is apart from God. It is the old fallen nature that still hinders every believer.

> **Now the works of the flesh are manifest, which are these; Adultery, fornication, uncleanness, lasciviousness, Idolatry, witchcraft, hatred, variance, emulations, wrath, strife, seditions, heresies, Envyings, murders, drunkenness, revellings, and such like: of the which I tell you before, as I have also told you in time past, that they which do such things shall not**

> **inherit the kingdom of God. (Galatians 5:19-21)**

Paul said that the works of the flesh are manifest. The word **manifest** carries the idea of *"unveiling, or exposing."* The way to identify the flesh is by its works. James is saying, *"I can identify the source by its symptoms."* Feuding and fussing is the result of yielding to the old depraved nature.

... the lusts that war in your members. This speaks of the war that rages in every Christian. There is an ongoing conflict that every Christ has to deal with as the two natures oppose one another.

> **For the flesh lusteth against the Spirit, and the Spirit against the flesh: and these are contrary the one to the other: so that ye cannot do the things that ye would. (Galatians 5:17)**

The word **lusteth** that Paul uses here is different from the word lust that James used. The word **lusteth** speaks of a strong desire. Paul states that the Spirit and the flesh lust **against** each other, meaning they have opposite desires for us. The flesh wants us to succumb to sin while the Spirit wants us to live for Christ. Paul goes on to say that **these are contrary the one to the other.** The word **contrary** means to *"oppose or confront."* The flesh dictates that we be one way and the Spirit immediately steps up and opposes the sinful nature and demands that we walk in the Spirit. The flesh and the Spirit are adversaries—they are enemies one of another. They are not going to compromise and they will never be at peace. The battle rages as these two adversaries fight to gain ground in the Christian's life. James identifies the cause of conflict as the flesh. There will always be war as long we are in this world. However, we can have victory.

> **This I say then, Walk in the Spirit, and ye shall not fulfil the lust of the flesh. (Galatians 5:16)**

God has promised us that:

> **... in all these things we are more than conquerors through him that loved us. (Romans 8:37)**

God people do not have to be defeated by the flesh. We are **more than conquerors.**

THE CHARACTERISTICS OF CONFLICT

Here James lays out some of the problems that result from worldly conflict in the Church.

UNSATISFIED PLEASURE

Ye lust, and have not ... (James 4:2a) This word lust means *"to set the heart upon; long for; covet; or desire."* When a man allows himself to desire something. That desire will eventually dominate his thoughts to the point that he lives in a state of dissatisfaction. We live in an unsatisfied society. The flesh drives depraved man to lust after Possessions, Prestige, Prominence, Position and Perversion. But he is never satisfied, the more he gets the more he wants. The madness for more only enslaves and ruins lives and ends in defeat. Jesus warned:

> **... Take heed, and beware of covetousness: for a man's life consisteth not in the abundance of the things which he possesseth. (Luke 12:15)**

After all the lust and desire, after all the heartache and hurt, James says, **Ye lust, and have not.** Lust never delivers what we want, it only brings more want and misery. Nothing of any lasting value comes from it. This is why God's people are admonished to, **Set your affection on things above, not on things on the earth. (Colossians 3:2)**

UNRESTRAINED PASSIONS

James says, **... ye kill, and desire to have, and cannot obtain: ye fight and war, yet ye have not, because ye ask not. (James 4:2b)** Lust can lead to other sins including murder. Absalom is a good example of this in his attempt to kill his father for the Kingdom (2 Samuel 15-17). David also was guilty of the same thing. He had Uriah killed so that he could have his wife. Ahab's desire for a vineyard resulted in the murder of Naboth (1 Kings 21:1-13). The idea is that covetousness results in deadly hatred and destructive behavior. You say, "Come on Preacher, I would never murder anyone." How about all that hatred you have stored up in your heart.

> **Whosoever hateth his brother is a murderer: and ye know that no murderer hath eternal life abiding in him. (1 John 3:15)**

James says, **and cannot obtain.** The word **obtain** means to *"take hold of," "make one's own," "grasp."* All the killing, fighting, and warring and they still couldn't get their hands on what they were after.

James says, **ye have not, because ye ask not.** We need to keep our eyes on the Lord and not on things of this world. God delights in providing for us. Jesus said,:

> **Ask, and it shall be given you; seek, and ye shall find; knock, and it shall be opened unto you: (Matthew 7:7)**

Notice that it is necessary for one to ask in order to receive, but the people James was writing to weren't asking.

UNANSWERED PRAYER

Ye ask, and receive not, because ye ask amiss, that ye may consume it upon your lusts. (James 4:3) Some were asking, but they were asking for selfish reasons. Why is it that we no longer see the great answers to prayer that we used to hear about. God still promises:

> **Call unto me, and I will answer thee, and shew thee great and mighty things, which thou knowest not. (Jeremiah 33:3)**

However, sin is a roadblock to answered prayer.

> **If I regard iniquity in my heart, the Lord will not hear me: (Psalms 66:18)**

The greatest need of the day is revival, yet there is no revival. Sin has shut up the Heavens. God promises in His Word to revive those who meet His conditions.

> **If my people, which are called by my name, shall humble themselves, and pray, and seek my face, and turn from their wicked ways; then will I hear from heaven, and will forgive their sin, and will heal their land. (2 Chronicles 7:14)**

This is a promise that great revivalists have claimed for years. Billy Sunday stood on the promises of God and saw great revival. D. L. Moody claimed the same promises and lived in revival. The same with George Whitfield, John Wesley, Charles Spurgeon, A. B. Earle, and countless others. Nothing has changed! There is only one question that needs to be answered. Are we willing to come on God's terms?

UNFAITHFUL PARTNERSHIP

Ye adulterers and adulteresses, know ye not that the friendship of the world is enmity with God? whosoever therefore will be a friend of the world is the enemy of God. Do ye think that the scripture saith in vain, The spirit that dwelleth in us lusteth to envy? (James 4:4-5) James addresses them as **adulterers and adulteresses**. This is strong language, but it is how God feels about those who forsake Him for the world. When a wife cheats on her husband it is called adultery because she has forsaken her relationship. When God's people fall into worldliness God considers it adultery. God said of His people Israel:

> ... the land hath committed great whoredom, departing from the LORD. (Hosea 1:2)

Later God said:

> My people ask counsel at their stocks, and their staff declareth unto them: for the spirit of whoredoms hath caused them to err, and they have gone a whoring from under their God. (Hosea 4:12)

Jesus used the same language referring to the unbelieving Jews of His day when He called them:

> **A wicked and adulterous generation ... (Matthew 16:4)**

When a believer forsakes God for the world, God sees it as adultery. This ought to arrest our attention. We need to look at our relationship with God as seriously as He does.

> **Love not the world, neither the things that are in the world. If any man love the world, the love of the Father is not in him. For all that is in the world, the lust of the flesh, and the lust of the eyes, and the pride of life, is not of the Father, but is of the world. And the world passeth away, and the lust thereof: but he that doeth the will of God abideth for ever. 1 (John 2:15-17)**

The world has become so churchy and the Church has become so worldly that you can hardly tell them apart. We have never seen a more religious world and we have never seen a more wicked churchianity. There is a sad lack of discernment among believers and the world has been brought into the Church. The devil could fold his horns back, tuck his tail in his pants and join the average Baptist Church. The world can steal our heart away from God.

For Demas hath forsaken me, having loved this present world ... (2 Timothy 4:10)

The world and the Church do not go together. We are to stay pure and loyal to God.

Do ye think that the scripture saith in vain, The spirit that dwelleth in us lusteth to envy? (James 4:5) This can be a tough verse to deal with. It is often taught that James is talking about the Holy Spirit's jealously over the believer's unfaithfulness to God. However, while that is a common interpretation, it is probably not the right one. The word **envy** comes from the Greek word *"phthonos"* and it has a negative connotation in Scripture. In his "Expository Dictionary of Bible Words," Renn says:

> *"Envy" is the dominant emotion motivating the Jewish leaders who sought to have Jesus handed over to the Roman courts in Matt. 27:18; Mark 15:10. "Envy" is listed among a number of vices in Rom. 1:29; Gal. 5:21; 1 Tim. 6:4; Titus 3:3; 1 Pet. 2:1. Phil. 1:15 affirms that some false teachers preach Christ out of "envy."*

This is not a word that is associated with God. A second thought that is important here is that James used the word **scripture**. What did he mean by scripture? Well, there was no New Testament at this time. James was referring to the Old Testament. There was no Old Testament teaching concerning the indwelling of the Holy Spirit. The indwelling ministry of the Spirit is particular only to this (the Church) dispensation. In the Old Testament God's people were not indwelt with the Holy Spirit. He came upon them to anoint and empower them for a specific calling, but He did not indwell them.

When James talks about the spirit that dwells in us lusting to envy, he is not talking about the Holy Spirit. He is talking about our human spirit. The spirit that dwells in me, my human spirit, has a natural tendency towards envy and jealousy. We have seen the **Cause of Conflict**, the **Characteristics of Conflict**, now James deals with ...

THE CURE FOR CONFLICT

We are not left without a remedy. James gives us a six-fold cure for dealing with conflict in the Church.

RELY ON GRACE

But he giveth more grace ... (James 4:6) That is the answer to our problems! More grace! This is not saving grace, as believers we already have that. Rather, this is **more grace**. This is not the grace that saves, but the grace that sustains. God's grace enables us to do what God requires. Oliver Greene used to say,

"What God demands, God provides." Paul wrote to Timothy:

> **... be strong in the grace that is in Christ Jesus. (2 Timothy 2:1)**

Such was Paul's testimony. He knew what it meant to live by the grace of God. These words were penned by Paul thirty years after his encounter with Christ on the Damascus road (Acts 9). For thirty years he had lived his life by the same grace that he was commanding others to live by. Paul had survived many trials and troubles by the grace of God. Even at the writing of these words to his young preacher boy, Paul was sitting in prison in Rome awaiting his execution.

> **Let us therefore come boldly unto the throne of grace, that we may obtain mercy, and find grace to help in time of need. (Hebrews 4:16)**

Notice that the grace of God is available **in time of need**—any need! God's people often fail because they focus on the problems of life instead of drawing upon God's provision of grace.

Relinquish Your Rights

Submit yourselves therefore to God ... (James 4.7a) The word **submit** comes from two words —*"under"* and *"to arrange."* It is a military term that means to *"arranges oneself under the commander."*

We are to arrange ourselves under God's authority. He is the commander and we are the soldiers.

No one accomplishes anything in the battle unless he follows the commander's instruction. Rebellion is one of the most frequently mentioned sins in the Bible. Rebellion always leads to judgment.

> **For rebellion is as the sin of witchcraft, and stubbornness is as iniquity and idolatry. Because thou hast rejected the word of the LORD, he hath also rejected thee from being king. And Saul said unto Samuel, I have sinned: for I have transgressed the commandment of the LORD, and thy words: because I feared the people, and obeyed their voice. (1 Samuel 15:23-24)**

Rebellion disregards God's authority and puts self on the throne. Nothing good ever comes out of rebellion; the result is always disastrous. **Submit yourselves therefore to God.**

Resist The Devil

Resist the devil, and he will flee from you. (James 4.7b) Here is a command with a promise. If we resist him he will eventually flee. After warning his reader about Satan Peter said, **Whom resist stedfast in the faith ... (1 Peter 5:9a)** We are commanded to resist the devil. The word resist is also a military term. It is a strong word that speaks of an all out determination to defeat the opposition. War is a life or death situation. You don't play around when you are in battle. Believers get into trouble when they don't take the battle seriously. Peter goes on to say that we accomplish this by being, **stedfast in the faith.** The word **stedfast** is also a military word. It means to be fixed and firm. It carries the idea of putting up a solid defense. We are to dig into a fixed and firm position and resist—we must hold our ground.

REPENT OF SIN

Draw nigh to God, and he will draw nigh to you. Cleanse your hands, ye sinners; and purify your hearts, ye double minded. (James 4:8) The words **draw nigh** mean to *"come near."* The idea is to approach someone. James challenges his readers to pursue fellowship with the Lord. The language here is that of the Levitical priest coming near the altar.

> **And let the priests also, which come near to the LORD, sanctify themselves, lest the LORD break forth upon them. (Exodus 19:22)**

It was a serious matter when the priest went before God on the day of atonement. He had to be right or he would die. James says, **Cleanse your hands, ye sinners; and purify your heart.** We learn in Exodus 30:17-21 that the priest had to wash his hands and feet at the laver. We need to have a clean life in order to fellowship with God.

> **Having therefore these promises, dearly beloved, let us cleanse ourselves from all filthiness of the flesh and spirit, perfecting holiness in the fear of God. (2 Corinthians 7:1)**

John said

> **If we confess our sins, he is faithful and just to forgive us our sins, and to cleanse us from all unrighteousness. (1 John 1:9)**

The whole idea here is that we must confess our sin if we are to draw nigh to God. We cannot fellowship with Him with unconfessed sin in our life.

Be afflicted, and mourn, and weep: let your laughter be turned to mourning, and your joy to heaviness. (James 4:9) This is the attitude of repentance. When we see our sin as God sees it, we will be broken. Genuine repentance involves grief over sin. When we get to this point we present ourselves to God as utterly helpless and broken. This is the idea behind Christ's words:

> **Blessed are the poor in spirit: for theirs is the kingdom of heaven. (Matthew 5:3)**

I understand that a believer can fall. However, it is contrary to the nature of the born again to live in sin as if its acceptable.

RENOUNCE YOUR PRIDE

Humble yourselves in the sight of the Lord, and he shall lift you up. (James 4:10) The word humble carries the idea of being low. When we see the greatness and majesty of God it ought to humble us. After Christ's miracle of the large catch of fish Peter:

> **... fell down at Jesus' knees, saying, Depart from me; for I am a sinful man, O Lord. (Luke 5:8)**

God hates pride (Proverbs 6) and we have nothing to be prideful about. Several Bible characters serve as examples of how God deals with pride. Cain (Genesis 4:3-16), Pharaoh (Exodus 5-15), Nebuchadnezzar (Daniel 4:29-33), and Herod (Acts 12:21-23). Charles Bridges wrote of pride:

> *There is no sin more abhorrent to his character. It is as if we were taking the crown from his head, and placing it upon our own. It is man making a god of himself.*

Pride is exalting one's self to the place of God. Solomon warned:

> **Only by pride cometh contention: but with the well advised is wisdom. (Proverbs 13:10)**

There will always be conflict where there is pride. Pride is a sin that is common to all men and women. God help us to humble ourselves in the sight of God.

REFRAIN YOUR TONGUE

Speak not evil one of another, brethren ... (James 4:11a) James turns again to the sin of the tongue. The words **speaketh evil** mean *"to defame, to denigrate, to slander."* The idea is that of running someone down. Some folks think that making others look small makes them look big.

... He that speaketh evil of his brother, and judgeth his brother, speaketh evil of the law, and judgeth the law: but if thou judge the law, thou art not a doer of the law, but a judge. There is one lawgiver, who is able to save and to destroy: who art thou that judgest another? (James 4:11b-12) The idea here is that the person who judges his brother is usurping God's authority. Only God has the ability to enforce his laws and carry out his purposes. A slanderous Christian attempts to play the role of God.

Failing To Put God Into Your Plans

James 4:13-17

In this section James deals with the tragedy of making plans and attempting to carry them out as if it were up to us. Sometimes times we count on tomorrow as if it is ours, yet tomorrow may not come as we expect it to. Too often plans are surmised, goals are set, life is spent with little or no concern for the will of God. Failing to put God into your plans results in …

A Selfish Life

Go to now, ye that say, To day or to morrow we will go into such a city, and continue there a year, and buy and sell, and get gain: (James 4:13) Here are the plans of a selfish person. It is a story of a life lived for self. Notice about midway of the verse the two little words, **we will.** It is not "God will," but we will. It is a life that has squeezed God out of its plans. They said, **we will go … and continue … and buy**

and sell, and get gain. Their plans reek with raw arrogance. They decided where they were going, when they will go, how long they will stay, and they are absolutely certain they will gain profit from their venture.

This verse describes a self-centered, selfish life with no regard for God. Many Christians live their life this way. They live as if there is no God. They are theological Christians, but practical atheists. They believe in God theologically, but in their daily practice they are atheist. They want nothing to do with God. They want to believe that they are saved, but want little or nothing to do with sanctification or service. Their life is all about their plans and desire rather than God's. There is nothing wrong with having plans or goals. However, the person who leaves God out of his plans is a fool. Failing to put God into your plans not only results in a **Selfish Life**, but also …

A Shallow Life

Whereas ye know not what shall be on the morrow. For what is your life? It is even a vapour, that appeareth for a little time, and then vanisheth away. (James 4:14) It is a shallow life because it is a life without God. It is lived and it is over. Nothing of any lasting value has come from it. They go on as if they have the world by the tail. They make big plans but James says, **ye know not what shall be on the**

morrow. There may not be a tomorrow. Solomon warned,

> **Boast not thyself of to morrow; for thou knowest not what a day may bring forth. (Proverbs 27:1)**

For what is your life? It is even a vapour, that appeareth for a little time, and then vanisheth away. James draws their attention to the brevity and uncertainty of life. Our Lord condemned this kind of presumptuous and selfish living.

> **And he spake a parable unto them, saying, The ground of a certain rich man brought forth plentifully: And he thought within himself, saying, What shall I do, because I have no room where to bestow my fruits? And he said, This will I do: I will pull down my barns, and build greater; and there will I bestow all my fruits and my goods. And I will say to my soul, Soul, thou hast much goods laid up for many years; take thine ease, eat, drink, and be merry. But God said unto him, Thou fool, this night thy soul shall be required of thee: then whose shall those things be, which thou hast provided? So is he that layeth up treasure for himself, and is not rich toward God. (Luke 12:16-21)**

Here is a man who was on top of the world. He had produced a bumper crop to the point that he didn't even have a place to store it. He had to tear down his barns and build bigger ones. He stored up everything he had and sat back to live the easy life. He would **eat, drink, and be merry.** But what startling words follow. **But God said unto him, Thou fool, this night thy soul shall be required of thee.** Someone wrote:

When as a child, I laughed and wept—TIME CREPT.

When as a youth, I dreamed and talked—TIME WALKED.

When I became a full-grown man — TIME RAN.

When older still I grew — TIME FLEW.

Soon I shall find in passing on—TIME GONE.

Time has a way of getting away from us. Failing to put God into our plans not only results in a **Selfish Life** and a **Shallow Life**, but also ...

A Seditious Life

For that ye ought to say, If the Lord will, we shall live, and do this, or that. (James 4:15) It is a seditious or rebellious life because God has been left out. It is sad that a lot of Christians have hijacked their own life. They have taken their life away from God and are living it the way they want to with no regard for God's will. These people had edged God out of their life. But the fact of life's uncertainty and the lack of knowledge concerning the future ought to drive us all the more to yield to the will of God. James encourages them to make God their main priority. We are to seek His will and do His will.

Jonah tried to blow off the will of God, but it didn't work. God caught up with him. It was Charles Spurgeon who said:

> *God never allows His Children to sin successfully.*

The greatest obstacle to a disobedient life is God Himself. The child of God may choose a life of sin and disobedience, but he will have to fight God all the way. Quit living as though God has no say in the matter. Seek His will and do it. The secret to being in the will of God tomorrow is to obey the will of God today.

Failing to put God into your plans results in a **Selfish Life**, a **Shallow Life**, a **Seditious Life** and ...

A Sinful Life

But now ye rejoice in your boastings: all such rejoicing is evil. (James 4:16) James describes those who live their lives apart from God as evil boasters. How sad! How deceived! For a man to brag about tomorrow's plans and supposed accomplishments when he has absolutely no control of the future is foolish. God holds tomorrow in His hands. He may or may or may not us another day. It is all according to His good pleasure. Solomon said:

> **Boast not thyself of to morrow; for thou knowest not what a day may bring forth. (Proverbs 27:1)**

Therefore to him that knoweth to do good, and doeth it not, to him it is sin. (James 4:17) To count on tomorrow to do what you know you ought to do today is not only foolish, it is sinful.

Wealth, Wages and Wrath

James 5:1-6

We all heard the old adage "Money Talks." Someone said, "If money talks, about the only thing it ever says to me is 'Goodbye.'" The fact of the matter is, money does talk. In fact, it speaks louder than words. There are at least four ways that our money talks. How we **<u>Get</u>** it; how we **<u>Guard</u>** it; how we **<u>Glory</u>** in it and how we **<u>Give</u>** it. Our money speaks volumes. What does your money say about you?

James does not condemn riches, nor does the Bible anywhere condemn anyone for being rich. The Bible speaks of several godly men who had riches in abundance, as Abraham, Job, Joseph, and others. These men were rich, but their money was not their god.

When it comes to possessions the Bible condemns covetousness and those who obtain and use their possessions sinfully. The Bible speaks against those who are rich in this worlds good, but are not rich toward God. God said to the rich farmer:

> ...Thou fool, this night thy soul shall be required of thee: then whose shall those things be, which thou hast provided? So is he that layeth up treasure for himself, and is not rich toward God. (Luke 12:20-21)

Here is a man who had it made. He had given his life for what he could gain. He had been successful. He finally had enough to retire. He had gathered much and said to himself:

> ... thou hast much goods laid up for many years; take thine ease, eat, drink, and be merry. (Luke 12:19)

What a retirement plan! He had it put together. He was set for life. His problem was that his life was going to run out that very night. There is nothing wrong with making plans, but we must remember that those plans are subject to God's approval.

> A man's heart deviseth his way: but the LORD directeth his steps. (Proverbs 16:9)

In the case this rich man, God interrupted his retirement plans and everything he had worked for went to someone else.

The rich men that James addressed had gotten their money by defrauding others. The Bible has a lot to say about riches and those who make money their god. Once money becomes your god you will do anything for it. We see here four truths concerning those whose money is their god.

THE SORROW OF UNSANCTIFIED RICHES

Go to now, ye rich men, weep and howl for your miseries that shall come upon you. (James 5:1) James starts with **Go to now...** This phrase means, "Listen up and pay attention." He sets out to get their attention from the start. James identifies those to whom he is speaking as **ye rich men**. James addresses those who have given their lives to what they could possess. Again, James is not condemning all rich people. The context shows that James is dealing with those who have made a god of their possessions.

James says, **weep and howl for your miseries that shall come upon you.** The words **weep and howl** are used in Scripture of those who have incurred the wrath and judgment of God. See Isaiah 15:3; Joel 1:5. The word **weep** means *"to sob and wail aloud."* The word **howl** carries the idea of *"shrieking, moaning and howling."* The words describe a situation of extreme and inescapable agony. Anyone who lives for money will experience misery. For most it will be an eternal misery and torment. The rich man in hell cried out:

> **...I am tormented in this flame. (Luke 16:24)**

This man had plenty of money and possessions while upon earth, but in he could afford a drop of water. He had life his life without God, not he is spending his eternity with Him. Hell is the ultimate payday of those who put their riches above their duty to God.

THE SPOILING OF UNSANCTIFIED RICHES

Your riches are corrupted, and your garments are motheaten. (James 5:2) Notice the terms **corrupted** and **motheaten**. The next verse talks about **cankered**, and **rust**. Such conditions plainly point to the fact that their possessions were not even in use. Most of what they owned was stored up and wasting away. These rich men had accumulated so much that it was rotting in their storehouses. The word **corrupted** comes from word that means *"putrefy or perish"* and used of spoiled food. They had robbed the workers who reaped the fields. Now the riches they gained were corrupted. Like spoiled food that was rotting away their riches could not be enjoyed.

James reminded them that their **garments** are **motheaten.** Expensive garments were the pride of the East. In Bible times a man's garments spoke of his wealth and social status. Joseph gave his brothers garments.

> To all of them he gave each man changes of raiment; but to Benjamin he gave three hundred pieces of silver, and five changes of raiment. (Genesis 45:22)

It was a fancy garment that caught Achan's attention and got him into trouble.

> When I saw among the spoils a goodly Babylonish garment, and two hundred shekels of silver, and a wedge of gold of fifty shekels weight, then I coveted them, and took them; and, behold, they are hid in the earth in the midst of my tent, and the silver under it. (Joshua 7:21)

Samson offered thirty changes of garments to anyone who could solve his riddle.

> And Samson said unto them, I will now put forth a riddle unto you: if ye can certainly declare it me within the seven days of the feast, and find it out, then I will give you thirty sheets and thirty change of garments: (Judges 14:12)

The rich loved to show their wealth by the way they dressed. You will remember that the rich man was clothed in **purple and fine linen**. The clothing of these rich men was stored away and being eaten by moths. They wouldn't even entertain the thought of giving them to the poor and needy.

James said, **Your gold and silver is cankered... (James 5:3)** The gold and silver which they had gathered up and hoarded was becoming rusty and tarnished. It had lost its luster. Like Aachen who took the wedge of gold, all he could do with it is burry it. Timothy warned:

> **Charge them that are rich in this world, that they be not highminded, nor trust in uncertain riches, but in the living God, who giveth us richly all things to enjoy; That they do good, that they be rich in good works, ready to distribute, willing to communicate; Laying up in store for themselves a good foundation against the time to come, that they may lay hold on eternal life. (1 Timothy 6:17-19)**

These wicked rich had hoarded everything they could gather and ignored the need of others.

James said, ... **and the rust of them shall be a witness against you, and shall eat your flesh as it were fire. Ye have heaped treasure together for the last days. (James 5:3b)** James warned them their rusty money would be a witness against them in the day of judgment. The fires of Hell do not settle down for money. Solomon said:

> **Riches profit not in the day of wrath ... (Proverbs 11:4)**

The rich man of Luke 16 was loaded with money while on earth, but in Hell he couldn't buy a few drops of water to cool his parched tongue. Jesus said:

> **Lay not up for yourselves treasures upon earth, where moth and rust doth corrupt, and where thieves break through and steal: But lay up for yourselves treasures in heaven, where neither moth nor rust doth corrupt, and where thieves do not break through nor steal: For where your treasure is, there will your heart be also. (Matthew 6:19-21)**

These rich men had stored up their wealth in the wrong place—here on earth!

THE SCOURGE OF UNSANCTIFIED RICHES

Behold, the hire of the labourers who have reaped down your fields, which is of you kept back by fraud ... (James 5:4a) These rich men had gotten their wealth by fraudulent means. James said, **the hire of the labourers ... is of you kept back by fraud.** The rich were cheating their workers out of their pay. Such a practice was forbidden.

> **Thou shalt not oppress an hired servant that is poor and needy, whether he be of thy brethren, or of thy strangers that are in thy land within thy gates: At his day thou shalt give him his hire, neither shall the sun go down upon it; for he is poor, and setteth his heart upon it: lest he cry against thee unto the LORD, and it be sin unto thee. (Deuteronomy 24:14-15)**

The rich care not how they get their money so long as they get it. People who are motivated by money go after it any way they can.

> **He that oppresseth the poor to increase his riches, and he that giveth to the rich, shall surely come to want. (Proverbs 22:16)**

Over and over in the word of God we are warned about the negative effects of money. Money can blind a person concerning the things of God and when a man sells out to money he loses his future. Jeremiah said:

> **As the partridge sitteth on eggs, and hatcheth them not; so he that getteth riches, and not by right, shall leave**

them in the midst of his days, and at his end shall be a fool. (Jeremiah 17:11)

James warns, **... the cries of them which have reaped are entered into the ears of the Lord of sabaoth. (James 5:4b)** Rest assured, God undertakes for the laborer who is cheated. God hears their cry and payday will be rough. God is called the **Lord of sabaoth.** It is the name for God that is usually translated **"Lord of Hosts."** This term is used in a military sense and speaks of God in all of His power as commander of Heaven's mighty forces.

Ye have lived in pleasure on the earth, and been wanton; ye have nourished your hearts, as in a day of slaughter. Ye have condemned and killed the just; and he doth not resist you. (James 5:5-6) These rich men lived in **pleasure on earth.** Notice the emphasis on **earth.** There will be no pleasure in the life to come. The word **wanton** speaks of pleasure and self-indulgence. They lived the very lap of luxury. They denied themselves nothing. Like the rich man of Luke 16, they:

> ... fared sumptuously every day. (Luke 16:19)

James says, **... ye have nourished your hearts, as in a day of slaughter.** What a startling picture we have here. James compares these labor-robbing, luxury-loving rich men to animals which are being fattened for the slaughter. These dumb animals, even on the very day of their slaughter, eat on and on as if they didn't have a care in the word. Riches blind people concerning the things of God and especially of His judgment.

Enduring With Patience

James 5:7-12

The Jewish believers to whom James was writing were living in difficult times. They suffered many problems and persecutions. They were hurting the situation seemed hopeless. It might have been easy to quit on God, but James encourages them to stay by the stuff and patiently wait for the Lord's return.

The Plea For Patience

Be patient therefore, brethren, unto the coming of the Lord. Behold, the husbandman waiteth for the precious fruit of the earth, and hath long patience for it, until he receive the early and latter rain. (James 5:7) Notice the word **therefore**. James is connecting what he is about to say to what he has just said. We saw in the last section that the rich had wronged others by cheating them out of their pay. But James warns that they are not to take matters into their own hands. Instead they are to operate according to Divine principle and wait on God. God's way is always the right way.

The word **patient** means to *"remain"* or *"abide under."* It is similar to the word **longsuffering** which is a fruit of the Spirit. The idea is that of endurance under affliction and provocation. The word is used to describe restraint and patience endurance, without anger or revenge, while suffering mistreatment. That is a hard thing to accomplish. Too often we seek revenge instead of waiting on the Lord. Jesus is a wonderful example of this kind of patience and longsuffering. When He could have summoned **more than twelve legions of angels (Matthew 26:53)** to His side, instead, **endured the cross. (Hebrews 12:2)** Later He prayed for their forgiveness.

> **Then said Jesus, Father, forgive them; for they know not what they do. (Luke 23:34)**

Christ is our example of patience and longsuffering. It is not easy to be patient in midst of trial. Our first instinct is usually to react in the flesh. However, God's plan is that we practice longsuffering and patience and let Him deal with the matter.

THE PROMISE WE POSSESS

Be ye also patient; stablish your hearts: for the coming of the Lord draweth nigh. Grudge not one

against another, brethren, lest ye be condemned: behold, the judge standeth before the door. (James 5:8-9) The promise of our Lord's imminent return encourages patience during trying times.

IT IS A CERTAIN RETURN

James speaks with absolute certainty when he says **... for the coming of the Lord draweth nigh.** He was speaking to believers about the rapture of the Church. He didn't say, "the Lord might return." He didn't say, "The Lord could return." He said, **the coming of the Lord draweth nigh.** The word **draweth** is in the present tense. God's plan is in motion as we speak. The return of Christ is imminent and certain. Notice that **the judge standeth before the door.** He could come through at any time. J. Vernon McGee points out:

> *The coming of Christ will correct the wrongs of the world. We can read this again and again in Scripture. Not only do the prophets mention it, but Christ Himself made it clear in the Sermon on the Mount (which will be the law of His kingdom) that He intends to give the poor a square deal under His reign (see Matt. 6:19-24).*

The Scriptures continually admonish believers to **watch, be ready,** and to expect His return **at a time when ye think not.** Though things weren't well with these believers that still had the **blessed hope. (Titus 2:13)** The imminent return is the hope of the Church. It is a **Certain Return**, and ...

IT IS A COMFORTING RETURN

James says, **stablish your hearts... (James 5:8)** Remember the context. James was writing to believers who were persecuted and facing trial after trial. Because of their faith these believers were suffering greatly. They had been driven from their homes, rejected by their families and lost everything they owned. On top of that, they were being cheated out of their pay. Why? Because they identified with Christ.

But James says **stablish your hearts...** The **stablish** means *"to fix; to settle in a state for permanence; to make firm."* James was telling them to settle down and keep their hearts fixed upon the Lord's return. Speaking of the rapture Paul said:

> **... wherefore comfort one another with these words. (1 Thessalonians 4:18)**

The rapture is a comforting prospect. This world is not our home. We are looking for the one to come. Peter had the same idea.

> **Wherein ye greatly rejoice, though now for a season, if need be, ye are in heaviness through manifold temptations: That the trial of your faith,**

> **being much more precious than of gold that perisheth, though it be tried with fire, might be found unto praise and honour and glory at the appearing of Jesus Christ: (1 Peter 1:6-7)**

Notice that the believer doesn't simply rejoice, but he can **greatly rejoice.** We can greatly rejoice though experiencing **manifold temptations.** The Word manifold means *"various"* or *"different kinds."* The idea is that no matter what comes at us we can still rejoice for it is only temporary. The rapture is the next great event in the redemptive plan and purpose of God. Our Lord will return literally and visibly, and summon His people with a shout like a trumpet blast. The graves of every dead saint will give up its dead and those still living at that time will be **caught up** with Christ to ever be with Him. That is our blessed hope. It is a **Certain Return**, it is a **Comforting Return**, and …

It Is A Challenging Return

Grudge not one against another, brethren, lest ye be condemned: behold, the judge standeth before the door. (James 5:9) James issues a strong challenge to live right. The return of Christ is one of the Christian's great incentives to holiness. One of the reasons folks live so wickedly is because they have no comprehension or they do not believe in the Lord's coming. If this world had a firm grip on the fact that

God will at any moment rapture His people out of this world and pour His judgment out on the wicked, there would be a lot less crime and wickedness out there. In the book of Luke He gave a parable teaching the importance of being ready for His any moment return.

> **But and if that servant say in his heart, My lord delayeth his coming; and shall begin to beat the menservants and maidens, and to eat and drink, and to be drunken; The lord of that servant will come in a day when he looketh not for him, and at an hour when he is not aware, and will cut him in sunder, and will appoint him his portion with the unbelievers. (Luke 12:45-46)**

Jesus is talking to a mixture of people here, including unbelievers, faithless believers, and believers who were not well informed as to the Lord's coming and His will. However, they all had one thing in common. They were saying, **My Lord delayeth his coming.** They were not expecting the Master's return and as a result were not living right. They were living as if they had plenty of time. Jesus said, **The lord of that servant will come in a day when he looketh not for him, and at an hour when he is not aware.** Many are saying today, just as the wicked and unfaithful steward, **My Lord delayeth his coming.**

(Luke 12:45) Too many look at the Lord's return as if He is not coming today. No wonder there is so much debauchery and defeat in the world today. However, He is coming and it could be today.

Sadly, many Christians have little or no concern for the coming judgment. They do not **Long** for His coming. They do not **Look** for His coming. Some do not even **Like** the idea of His coming. In essence they are saying, **My Lord delayeth his coming.** As a result many professing believers live like the world. But let us not forget that there is a judgment of the believer also. At the same time the world is being judged, believers will be judged in Heaven. That is why Martin Luther said:

> *I preach as though Christ died yesterday, rose from the dead today and was coming back tomorrow.*

Let not the child of God think that he can live like the Devil because he is eternally secure. Every believer must face the Lord and give an account of his life. The Bible declares that **we must all appear before the judgment seat of Christ... (2 Corinthians 5:10a)** What a challenge to live a holy life. A life pleasing to our Lord. Dr. R. A. Torrey said:

> *"The imminent return of our Lord is the greatest Bible argument for a pure, unselfish, devoted, unworldly, active life*

of service." The great Bible expositor, Dr. Campbell Morgan said, *"I never lay my head upon the pillow without thinking that maybe before the morning breaks, the final morning may have dawned. I never begin my work in the morning without thinking that perhaps He may interrupt my work and begin His own. We are not looking for death. We are looking for Him."*

There is no greater incentive to living a sanctified life than the imminent return of Christ.

THE PATTERN WE PURSUE

Take, my brethren, the prophets, who have spoken in the name of the Lord, for an example of suffering affliction, and of patience. (James 5:10) Having exhorted believers to stay by the stuff, James offers some Old Testament examples of those who had suffered great affliction, but endured with patience. He mentions **the prophets, who have spoken in the name of the Lord…** We consider men like Moses, Elijah, David, Daniel and numerous others. All of them suffered greatly for the Lord's cause. We need not think it to be strange that the godly suffer.

> Yea, and all that will live godly in Christ Jesus shall suffer persecution. (2 Timothy 3:12)

Jesus said:

> If the world hate you, ye know that it hated me before it hated you. If ye were of the world, the world would love his own: but because ye are not of the world, but I have chosen you out of the world, therefore the world hateth you. Remember the word that I said unto you, The servant is not greater than his lord. If they have persecuted me, they will also persecute you; if they have kept my saying, they will keep yours also. (John 15:18-20)

Jesus made reference to the suffering and persecution of the Prophets.

> O Jerusalem, Jerusalem, thou that killest the prophets, and stonest them which are sent unto thee, how often would I have gathered thy children together, even as a hen gathereth her chickens under her wings, and ye would not! (Matthew 23:37)

Such persecution continued into the Church age. Just before he was stoned to death, Stephen rebuked the Jews for their treatment of the Prophets.

> **Which of the prophets have not your fathers persecuted? and they have slain them which shewed before of the coming of the Just One; of whom ye have been now the betrayers and murderers: (Acts 7:52)**

Behold, we count them happy which endure. Ye have heard of the patience of Job, and have seen the end of the Lord; that the Lord is very pitiful, and of tender mercy. (James 5:11) James calls our attention to Job as an illustration of patient endurance. Job is good example of a man who suffered greatly, yet trusted and stayed true to God. Job lost everything. Job's affliction is seen in …

- ★ <u>**The Death of his Family**</u>
- ★ <u>**The Destruction of his Farm**</u>
- ★ <u>**The Decline of his Finances**</u>
- ★ <u>**The Disease in his Flesh**</u> and
- ★ <u>**The Disappointment by his Friends.**</u>

It seemed for job as though life was over. He lost it all. His wife suggested that he **curse God, and die. (Job 2:9)** Many would have taken her advice, but Job stayed by the stuff. Job endured with patience when he said:

> **Naked came I out of my mother's womb, and naked shall I return thither: the LORD gave, and the LORD hath taken away; blessed be the name of the LORD. In all this Job sinned not, nor charged God foolishly. (Job 1:21-22)**

Job endured with patience when he said:

> **Though he slay me, yet will I trust in him …(Job 13:15)**

Job endured with patience when he said:

> **For I know that my redeemer liveth, and that he shall stand at the latter day upon the earth: (Job 19:25)**

Job endured with patience when he said:

> **But he knoweth the way that I take: when he hath tried me, I shall come forth as gold. (Job 23:10)**

What an example to follow. God help us to endure with patience.

The Purity We Practice

But above all things, my brethren, swear not, neither by heaven, neither by the earth, neither

by any other oath: but let your yea be yea; and your nay, nay; lest ye fall into condemnation. (James 5:12) Our word is to be honest and straightforward. This is why James commands his readers to stop swearing by oaths. People with integrity do not need to swear by an oath because, having kept their word in the past, people believe what they say. God's concern is how we communicate in our ordinary conversations. In times of duress and stress, it is easy to make a false pledge. God desires that we be genuine in what we say rather than attaching a rash promise to our statement. Integrity should always guard our speech.

Prayer For The Hurting

James 5:13-18

We live in a world of hurting people. Many folks barely survive from day to day. They have little or no hope in this world. Our Saviour was drawn to the down and out. He said:

> **The Spirit of the Lord is upon me, because he hath anointed me to preach the gospel to the poor; he hath sent me to heal the brokenhearted, to preach deliverance to the captives, and recovering of sight to the blind, to set at liberty them that are bruised, (Luke 4:18)**

Jesus was drawn to the poor, the brokenhearted, the captives, the blind, the bruised. Jesus set the example for the Church to follow. James instructs us to pray for the sick and hurting.

Prayer And Suffering

Is any among you afflicted? let him pray. Is any merry? let him sing psalms. (James 5:13) The word

afflicted comes from the two Greek words, *"kako"* meaning *"evil,"* and *"patheia"* meaning *"to suffer."* James used this word in verse 10 speaking of the Old Testament Prophets **suffering affliction**. This is the word Paul used to described his persecution when he said:

I suffer trouble ... (2 Timothy 2:9)

It's the same word Paul used when he told Timothy to:

... endure afflictions. (2 Timothy 4:5)

This word describes persecution and suffering. How are we to handle such trouble? We are to pray! Not whine! Not quit! We are to pray! Times of affliction are times for prayer.

Prayer Will Keep Us Settled

Be careful for nothing; but in every thing by prayer and supplication with thanksgiving let your requests be made known unto God. And the peace of God, which passeth all understanding, shall keep your hearts and minds through Christ Jesus. (Philippians 4:6-7) Paul says pray about your circumstances rather than worrying about it. Paul said, **be careful for nothing.** Do not fear, do not fret, do not focus on your circumstances—God is in control. The word **careful** comes from a word that conveys the idea of *"being distracted"* or *"divided."* Worry distracts our mind and divides our heart. God can't do much with a divided heart. The Bible says a great deal about the whole heart as opposed to the divided heart (Psalm 9:1; 111:1; 119:2; 119:10; 119:34; 19:58; 119:69; 119:145; 138:1, Isaiah 1:5, Jeremiah 3:10; 24:7; 32:41).

Paul says, **but in every thing by prayer and supplication with thanksgiving let your requests be made known unto God.** We can't handle it but God can! Has God ever let you down? Have you ever given Him a problem that He did not have the ability to deal with? Did you ever ask Him for bread and get a stone? Did you ever ask Him for a fish and get a serpent? Absolutely not! God is bigger than our problems! There is nothing too great for Him. Our God doesn't cut corners or come up short. In every situation He is sufficient to meet every need.

> **Ah Lord GOD! behold, thou hast made the heaven and the earth by thy great power and stretched out arm, and there is nothing too hard for thee. (Jeremiah 32:17)**

Notice Paul says, **in every thing**. That includes little things as well as big things. We are to take everything to God. When we do we are assured that **the peace of God, which passeth all understanding, shall keep your hearts and minds through Christ Jesus.**

Christians will never have peace as long as they are distracted by their problems.

Prayer Will Keep Us Strong

In the day when I cried thou answeredst me, and strengthenedst me with strength in my soul. (Psalm 138:3) David sought the Lord and the Lord heard and answered. There was no delay. David called and God answered! How many times can we testify **when I cried thou answeredst me.** Too often we enjoy the gift and forget the Giver! David said God answered **and strengthenedst me with strength in my soul.** That is a significant statement! Notice that David was strengthened in his soul. We need physical strength, but there is a greater need for spiritual strength. Our heart must be strengthened. The Psalmist said:

> **I had fainted, unless I had believed to see the goodness of the LORD in the land of the living. Wait on the LORD: be of good courage, and he shall strengthen thine heart: wait, I say, on the LORD. (Psalms 27:13-14)**

Paul prayed for the Ephesians to be:

> **... strengthened with might by his Spirit in the inner man; (Ephesians 3:16)**

The Christian life is lived from the heart—if we are not strong in the inner man, in our soul, we will fail at living for Christ.

Prayer Will Keep Us Serving

The book of Nehemiah serves as a powerful example of this truth. The work of rebuilding the walls around Jerusalem had begun and progress was being made. The enemies were furious because God's people were moving forward.

> **But it came to pass, that when Sanballat heard that we builded the wall, he was wroth, and took great indignation, and mocked the Jews. (Nehemiah 4:1)**

There is always going to be opposition to the Lord's work. James has already told us in chapter one to **_Expect_** it, **_Endure_** it and **_Enjoy_** it. God's people were making great progress and look at the enemies.

> **But it came to pass, that when Sanballat, and Tobiah, and the Arabians, and the Ammonites, and the Ashdodites, heard that the walls of Jerusalem were made up, and that the breaches began to be stopped, then they were very wroth. (Nehemiah 4:7)**

Notice three truths here..

1) in verse one it was **Sanballat** was alone. However, in verse seven it is **Tobiah, the Arabians, the Ammonites** and **the Ashdodites**. Any fool can gather a following if he hollers long and loud enough. That is why the Bible commands us to, **Answer a fool according to his folly, lest he be wise in his own conceit. (Proverbs 26:5)**

2) Notice in verse one that Sanbalat was **wroth**, but as God's people progress the enemies of God are **very wroth**. The enemy went from **wroth** to **very wroth** in a short amount of time. The anger of the enemy usually escalates as God gives His people victory.

3) **And conspired all of them together to come and to fight against Jerusalem, and to hinder it. (Nehemiah 4:8)** The enemies will join forces in an attempt to stop the work of God, but they will fail. Solomon said, **Though hand join in hand, the wicked shall not be unpunished: but the seed of the righteous shall be delivered. (Proverbs 11:21)** The phrase **hand join in hand** is an expression that speaks of shaking hands to agree on a matter. The enemies can get together and vow to stop God's work, but they need to realize that **the wicked shall not be unpunished** and **seed of the righteous shall be delivered.**

Nehemiah says, **Nevertheless we made our prayer unto our God ... (Nehemiah 4:9)** In the midst of danger and difficulty Nehemiah and the workers cried out to God and look at the result.

> **And it came to pass, when our enemies heard that it was known unto us, and God had brought their counsel to nought, that we returned all of us to the wall, every one unto his work. (Nehemiah 4:15)**

Not only does Prayer keep us **Settled**, and **Strong**, and **Serving**, but ...

Prayer Will Keep Us Sweet

> **At my first answer no man stood with me, but all men forsook me: I pray God that it may not be laid to their charge. Notwithstanding the Lord stood with me, and strengthened me; that by me the preaching might be fully known, and that all the Gentiles might hear: and I was delivered out of the mouth of the lion. (2 Timothy 4:16-17)**

Demas and others had forsaken Paul, but Paul asks that no blame be laid to their charge. Prayer keeps bitterness from gripping our heart. Our natural tendency is to get bitter towards people. The way of the flesh is to say, *"I'll get even."* But Paul was willing to forgive and forget about it. He did not need his pound of flesh. That is the mark of a great man.

> **And the LORD turned the captivity of Job, when he prayed for his friends: also**

the LORD gave Job twice as much as he had before. (Job 42:10)

Job's so-called friends had forsaken him but he kept a sweet spirit about it. A good prayer life will keep you sweet and serving even in the toughest of times.

Prayer Will Keep Us Singing

And at midnight Paul and Silas prayed, and sang praises unto God: and the prisoners heard them. (Acts 16:25) Here they were secured in the stocks and locked up, but they were praying and praising God. In a situation where many would have lost heart Paul and Silas cut loose and let the glory roll. They were singing and praying an having a time when:

> **… suddenly there was a great earthquake, so that the foundations of the prison were shaken: and immediately all the doors were opened, and every one's bands were loosed. (Acts 16:26)**

Talk about Jailhouse Rock! God came to town and it started with their praying and singing. Notice the last part of verse 25, it says **and the prisoners heard them.** The world needs to hear us singing when we face our trials. The old Methodist, John Nelson, was flung into a filthy dungeon at Bradford. He said, *"My soul was so filled with the love of God that it was a paradise to me. I wished my enemies were as happy in* *their houses as I was in the dungeon.*" A solid prayer life will help you to praise God in the tough times. Paul and Silas turn their situation into a worship service. And when they worshipped, God worked.

Prayer And Sickness

Is any sick among you? let him call for the elders of the church; and let them pray over him, anointing him with oil in the name of the Lord: And the prayer of faith shall save the sick, and the Lord shall raise him up; and if he have committed sins, they shall be forgiven him. (James 5:14-15) Unfortunately, this little passage of Scripture is surrounded with controversy. Faith healers often use this passage to promote their agenda. Roman Catholicism has laid claim to this text in an attempt to defend their teachings of "Extreme Unction" and "Confession to a Priest." However, this passage lends no support whatsoever to these groups and their doctrines. Let's break this passage down phrase by phrase and learn what James is teaching.

The Condition Of The Hurting

James starts out by asking the question, **Is any sick among you? (James 5:14a)** From the context, what James seems to be dealing with are believers who become sick due to unrepentant sinfulness. The context supports this view. James even says, **if he have committed sins, they shall be forgiven him. (James**

5:15) James also warned that some had gone to the point that they were on the brink of committing the sin unto death (James 5:20). Sin does cause illness and often leads to death. This was the case in the Corinthians Church. Some of them had observed the Lord's supper in an unworthy manner. In Paul's letter to them he wroteL

> **For this cause many are weak and sickly among you, and many sleep. (1 Corinthians 11:30)**

The Apostle John also dealt with this issue.

> **If any man see his brother sin a sin which is not unto death, he shall ask, and he shall give him life for them that sin not unto death. There is a sin unto death: I do not say that he shall pray for it. All unrighteousness is sin: and there is a sin not unto death. (1 John 5:16-17)**

There are several Bible examples of those who committed the sin unto death. Nadab and Abihu committed the sin unto death (Leviticus 10:1-2). Korah died the sin unto death (Numbers 16:31-34). Achan sinned a sin unto death (Joshua 7). Uzzah's sin resulted in death (2 Samuel 6:1-7). Ananias and Sapphira committed a sin unto death (Acts 5).

The **sin unto death** is the physical death which occurs when a Christian refuses to repent under the chastening hand of God.

> **He, that being often reproved hardeneth his neck, shall suddenly be destroyed, and that without remedy. (Proverbs 29:1)**

There is no determined period of time. It might be six months, one year, or ten years. It is entirely at God's discretion. He alone decides when enough is enough. He may give one opportunity to repent or a dozen. We do not know. That is why it is so important to accept correction when God convicts us.

> **Wherefore as the Holy Ghost saith, To day if ye will hear his voice, Harden not your hearts, as in the provocation, in the day of temptation in the wilderness. (Hebrews 3:7-8)**

The hardening effect of sin leads to death. However, not all sickness is due to sin. Some sickness is self-induced. Studies show that a large number, upwards to 50% of sickness is actually psychological. They have a real infirmity. Their symptoms are psychosomatic. Their illness is self-induced.

God sometimes allows sickness. Many folks have a problem with this one. You will remember the blind man back in John 9. The disciples asked Jesus which of the parents sinned and caused this man's blindness.

> **Jesus answered, Neither hath this man sinned, nor his parents: but that the works of God should be made manifest in him. (John 9:2-3)**

The man was born blind so that God could demonstrate His power.

Paul was given a thorn in the flesh in order to keep him humble.

> **And lest I should be exalted above measure through the abundance of the revelations, there was given to me a thorn in the flesh, the messenger of Satan to buffet me, lest I should be exalted above measure. (2 Corinthians 12:7)**

Nothing reminds us of our true abilities and worth quite like having to deal with an infirmity. Often God does not remove the thorn because it is beneficial to us. But Praise God he does give grace to deal with it.

THE CALL FOR THE ELDERS

The sick are to **call for the elders of the church. (James 5:14b)** The word elders is used two ways in Scripture. First, it speaks of the Pastor. He is the leader of the local church. He is to be someone who is grounded in faith and truth with the maturity and wisdom to deal with the problems of life (Acts 14:23; 20:17; 1 Timothy 5:17; Titus 1:5). So the sick are to call for the Pastor. Secondly, the word elder also applies to men in the local Church who are grounded and mature in their faith. The discernment and support of such men are invaluable to the Pastor.

Notice that the elders do not call for the sick. Besides being wrong in their interpretation of this passage, many get this thing backwards. They run around all over the place having their so-called "healing services" calling for the sick to come and get healed. They are out of order. The elders are not told to call for the sick, but for the sick to call for the elders..

There is another thought here. Often times folks get mad at the Pastor because he failed to visit them when they were sick. But notice that the sick are to call for the Elders. It is the responsibility of the sick to request a visit. The Pastor does not get a divine revelation every time one of the Church members gets sick. The sick need to call and the Pastor is be ready to respond if a visit is requested.

THE COMMAND TO PRAY

The elders' instructions concerning the sick is to **pray over him, anointing him with oil in the name of the Lord: (James 5:14c)** There is a three-fold responsibility here.

First, the elders are to go to the sick person's home and pray over him. Prayer is the Christian's spiritual strategy. Paul spoke of, **Praying always with all prayer and supplication in the Spirit. (Ephesians 6:18)** Prayer moves the hand and heart of God. Robert Hall said, *"The prayer of faith is the only power in the universe to which the Great Jehovah yields. Prayer is the sovereign remedy."* Prayer not only brings God into the matter, but it greatly encourages the sick.

Secondly, **anointing him with oil.** There are various ideas concerning the oil. Some believe it to be medicinal. Oil was a popular medicine in Bible days. However, it was for cuts, scrape and bruises. It would never help heart disease, cancer, pneumonia or any serious sickness. Oil in this passage is not medicinal.

Another view is that the oil is sacramental. Catholicism teaches that is talking about their sacrament of extreme unction. They will come in and anoint the sick with oil. Their claim is that even if the sick are not healed that their sins are forgiven. This passage does not support extreme unction. The oil here is not sacramental.

Another view and I believe to be the correct one, is that oil in the Bible is often symbolic of the Holy Spirit. When Aaron was made high priest, he was anointed with oil. God said:

> **Thou shalt take the anointing oil, and pour it upon his head, and anoint him. (Exodus 29:7)**

When Samuel anointed Saul with oil to become Israel's first king, we read:

> **The spirit of God came upon him. (1 Samuel 10:1, 10)**

Likewise, when Samuel anointed David,

> **The spirit of the LORD came upon David from that day forward. (1 Samuel 16:13)**

The anointing with oil was symbolic of the presence and power of the Holy Spirit. If there is healing it is not up to the elders. The elders have no special gift or powers. It is the Holy Spirit who touches people's lives and brings healing.

The Consequences Of Faith

And the prayer of faith shall save the sick, and the Lord shall raise him up; and if he have committed sins, they shall be forgiven him. (James 5:15) He says that it is also the prayer of faith that shall save the sick. It is not the oil that heals. It is not a medicine, it is not a sacrament and it is not a "divine healer." The prayer of faith connects with Heaven. I heard the story of a young lawyer who had just opened up a new office. There he sat behind his shiny new desk, eagerly awaiting his first client. Soon he heard footsteps in the hall and then a hand on the doorknob. Wanting to look important he pretended to be busy, so he picked up the telephone and carried on a fake conversation. "Yes, I'll have my secretary take care of that right away. I have a very tight schedule. Call me back in a few days." A man stepped through the door, listening to one end of the lawyers conversation. The lawyer hung up the phone and looked at what he hoped was a new client and said, "What may I do for you?" The man answered, "I'm from the phone company, and I here to connect your telephone." We have to be careful that our prayer life is not like that— mere talk with no connection. We must get a hold of Heaven if we are to see the miraculous. Charles Trumbull said, *"Prayer is releasing the energies of God. For prayer is asking God to do what we cannot do."*

And the prayer of faith shall save the sick, and the Lord shall raise him up; and if he have committed sins, they shall be forgiven him. (James 5:15) Notice here that it is not the oil that heals, but the **prayer of faith.** Divine healers get this one wrong also. When one of their victims fail to get healed it is always claimed that the person coming for healing didn't have enough faith. However, we see here it not the faith of the person coming, but the faith of the ones praying.

So then what is **the prayer of faith** that heals the sick? I believe it is found in the first epistle of John.

> **And this is the confidence that we have in him, that, if we ask any thing according to his will, he heareth us: And if we know that he hear us, whatsoever we ask, we know that we have the petitions that we desired of him. (1 John 5:14-15)**

Notice three important truths here.

First, **<u>the Confidence.</u>** **And this is the confidence that we have in him.** The word **confidence** means boldness and carries the idea of *"freedom of speech."* Praise God! We can have boldness when we come before God in prayer.

> **Let us therefore come boldly unto the throne of grace, that we may obtain mercy, and find grace to help in time of need" (Hebrews 4:16).**

We must understand that prayer is both a privilege and a command. Jesus said, **"men ought always to pray, and not to faint" (Luke 18:1).** Too many are becoming faint and failing in their walk for Christ. The word faint means to be weak or weary and carries the idea of being exhausted. Jesus put His finger on one of man's biggest prayer problems. One of the reasons for failure in the Christian life is trying to labor apart from prayer. Prayer makes God a partner in our work. Jesus said, **"without me ye can do nothing" (John 15:5)**. My friend, if you do not have confidence in prayer, you will faint in the work.

Second, **<u>the Condition</u>**. John further explains that our confidence is conditional. He adds, **"if we ask any thing according to his will, he heareth us."** You will notice the biggest little word in the English language—the word **"if."** Surely God will answer prayer, but there are conditions to be met. One of those conditions is clearly set forth here. We must ask **"according to his will."** The first fundamental of prayer is that we must ask according to God's will. However, before we can ask His will we must know His will and the only way to know the will of God is to spend time with Him in His Word. In other words, this promise of answered prayer is for those who are delighting themselves in the Lord and walking in fellowship with Him.

> **Delight thyself also in the LORD; and he shall give thee the desires of thine heart. Commit thy way unto the LORD; trust also in him; and he shall bring it to pass. (Psalm 37:4-5)**

The condition of answered prayer is that we delight ourselves in the Lord, commit ourselves to His ways. We must live according to the Word of God in order to enjoy answered prayer. John said earlier:

> **And whatsoever we ask, we receive of him, because we keep his commandments, and do those things that are pleasing in his sight. (1 John 3:22)**

If we are walking according to His will, then we will ask the right things of Him. That is, if we are delighting in Him, we will ask only those things that are pleasing to Him. Here is the bottom line. If our Lord prayed, **"Not my will, but Thine be done" (Luke 22:42)**, surely we should follow His example and seek only those things that fall within the boundaries of His will.

Third, <u>**the Courage**</u>. **And if we know that he hear us, whatsoever we ask, we know that we have the petitions that we desired of him.** John said, **if we know that he hear us.** Many are defeated in their prayer life because they do not have the confidence that God will answer their prayer. Walking in the will of God will build your prayer life and your faith as God answers your prayer.

PRAYER AND SERVICE

> **Elias was a man subject to like passions as we are, and he prayed earnestly that it might not rain: and it rained not on the earth by the space of three years and six months. And he prayed again, and the heaven gave rain, and the earth brought forth her fruit. (James 5:17-18)** Now to illustrate the faithful

prayer life, James goes back into the Old Testament to Elijah the Prophet. Elijah was a great hero in Jewish history. One thing you find about Elijah is that he was a man of God. He walked with God and he displayed the power of God in his life. He was serious about the things of God. Because Elijah walked with God, he could talk with God. The Bible says:

> **If I regard iniquity in my heart, the Lord will not hear me. (Psalms 66:18)**

Sin gets in the way of God answering prayer. We need so desperately to have our prayer answered, but sin hinders a Holy God from hearing us.

> **But your iniquities have separated between you and your God, and your sins have hid his face from you, that he will not hear. (Isaiah 59:2)**

We must learn to keep short accounts with God.

James tells us that Elijah **was a man subject to like passions as we are.** Elijah was made out of the same stuff you and I are made of. He was a man with problems, pains and perils. Yet he got a hold of Heaven and God moved on earth at Elijah's request. Notice the characteristics of Elijah's prayer.

IT WAS SERIOUS PRAYER

Elijah **prayed earnestly**. The word **earnestly** conveys the idea that Elijah "prayed with prayer" It is a strong word that means he prayed with great intensity and fervency. He put himself into his prayer.

IT WAS SCRIPTURAL PRAYER

We are told that Elijah, **prayed earnestly that it might not rain: and it rained not on the earth by the space of three years and six months. And he prayed again, and the heaven gave rain, and the earth brought forth her fruit. (James 5:17-18)** Elijah prayed for the closing of Heaven and it closed. He prayed for Heaven to open and God open it. Why was Elijah so powerful in his prayer life. He was powerful because he was Scriptural. Elijah prayed in accordance with God's word. God had declared that He would shut the Heavens and the skies would become as brass and the earth as iron if His people forsook Him.

> **And thy heaven that is over thy head shall be brass, and the earth that is under thee shall be iron. The LORD shall make the rain of thy land powder and dust: from heaven shall it come down upon thee, until thou be destroyed ... Thou shalt carry much seed out into the field, and shalt gather but little in; for the locust shall consume it. Thou shalt plant vineyards, and dress them, but shalt neither drink of the wine, nor gather the grapes; for the worms shall**

> eat them. Thou shalt have olive trees throughout all thy coasts, but thou shalt not anoint thyself with the oil; for thine olive shall cast his fruit. (Deuteronomy 28:23-24, 38-40)

God often removes His blessings in order to get our attention. Elijah prayed that God would shut the Heavens and get His people's attention.

It Was Successful Prayer

God used Elijah as His human instrument to get the attention of a backslidden nation and turn His people back to Him. That is success. R. A. Torrey said:

> *"Prayer is the key that opens wide the inexhaustible storehouse of divine grace and power. There is only one limit to what prayer can do; that is what God can do."*

To try living a life of victory and service apart from prayer is foolish and futile. The Christian who desires to know Christ more intimately and have power in his Christian life must pray consistently. **Call unto me, and I will answer thee, and shew thee great and mighty things, which thou knowest not. (Jeremiah 33:3)**

Restoring The Wayward

James 5:19-20

In this closing section James deals with one of the forgotten doctrines of Fundamentalism. That is the doctrine of restoration. We find here that it is the duty of every believer to attempt to restore the fallen. Jesus said,:

> **What man of you, having an hundred sheep, if he lose one of them, doth not leave the ninety and nine in the wilderness, and go after that which is lost, until he find it? And when he hath found it, he layeth it on his shoulders, rejoicing. (Luke 15:4-5)**

Notice four steps here:

1) <u>***The Reality***</u>. Jesus asked, **What man of you, having an hundred sheep, if he lose one of them...** This is a reality. God people do wander and before they know it, they are away from the Lord.

2) <u>***The Reclaiming***</u>. The Shepherd would **leave the ninety and nine** and go out and search for one

that was lost. He is not going to come back by himself. We need to go after him.

3) **_The Resolve_**. The shepherd would search **"until He find it."** Restoring the wayward requires a great deal of energy and work. It requires Desire, Determination, Diligence and Discipline.

4) **_The Rejoicing_**. **And when he hath found it, he layeth it on his shoulders, rejoicing. (Luke 15:5)** Once the lost sheep is found the rejoicing starts.

Yes, we are our brother's keeper. This responsibility of restoration is just as important and serious as soul-winning. Let's look at James' teaching on Going After The Wayward.

A Subtle Danger

Brethren, if any of you do err from the truth … (James 5:19) James is addressing the **Brethren** here. The word brethren is found over two hundred times in the New Testament. It is a term that is applied to those who are born into the family of God. That this passage is speaking of Christians is further seen in the phrase **err from the truth.** These are folks who have embraced the truth. They have heard it and they have received it. The word **err** comes from the word *"planao"* and simply means *"to wander."* It is the word from which we get planet. A planet is a wandering body. James is talking about people who are saved, but they have wandered off from the things of God. It is a sad fact that all over the world you can find people who trusted the Lord Jesus as their Saviour. They use to attended Church. Some used to preach the word. Some taught in Sunday-School. Some ushered. Some would sing specials. Many of them had places of service, but they have erred from the truth.

A Serious Duty

James says **and one convert him; Let him know, that he which converteth the sinner from the error of his way ... (James 5:19b-20a)** This is our duty. The word convert here is not used in the sense of being converted from a lost state. The Greek word is *"epistrephō" and means "to convert," "turn"* and *"return."* The idea is that of a brother or sister having wandered off from the truth. They are going in the wrong direction and need to be turned around. Jesus used this word when dealing with Peter.

> **But I have prayed for thee, that thy faith fail not: and when thou art converted, strengthen thy brethren. (Luke 22:32)**

Peter was getting ready to blow it big. He was going to wander off from the Lord. He had too much confidence in his own strength and stability. He thought he was superior to others.

> **Though all men shall be offended because of thee, yet will I never be offended. (Matthew 26:33)**

When we get to the place to where we think ourselves superior to others—we are in for a fall.

> **Wherefore let him that thinketh he standeth take heed lest he fall. (1 Corinthians 10:12)**

Peter messed up for sure. He denied the Lord and followed him afar off even cussing when they pressed him about it. You would never have known he was a Christian. There he was cussing and hanging with the world warming himself by their fire. He wander off. In addition to all that a few days later he quit on Jesus altogether. He flat left the ministry.

> **There were together Simon Peter, and Thomas called Didymus, and Nathanael of Cana in Galilee, and the sons of Zebedee, and two other of his disciples. Simon Peter saith unto them, I go a fishing. They say unto him, We also go with thee. They went forth, and entered into a ship immediately; and that night they caught nothing. (John 21:2-3)**

Peter ditched everything that the Lord had given him to do. He left it all in the dust when he went back to his old life. He backslid, but there was hope. Jesus said, **when thou art converted, strengthen thy brethren.** The thing we have to realize is that our Lord doesn't give up on the runaways. On the resurrection morning Jesus instructed the three women at the tomb,

> **But go your way, tell his disciples and Peter that he goeth before you into Galilee: there shall ye see him, as he said unto you. (Mark 16:7)**

Peter messed up, but he was still dear to the Lord. God still had a purpose for him. Jesus looked beyond Peter's failure to a successful ministry. Failure is not final. Paul also deals with the issue of restoration.

> **Brethren, if a man be overtaken in a fault, ye which are spiritual, restore such an one in the spirit of meekness; considering thyself, lest thou also be tempted. (Galatians 6:1)**

It speaks of one being **overtaken in a fault**. Overtaken comes from the word *"prolambano"* and carries the idea of *"taken by surprise."* The idea is that the fault catches the individual by surprise and suddenly. Before he knows what happened the fault has seized him. That is what happens when you flirt with sin. You get taken by surprise. The word restore was used in the medical world to speak of setting broken bones. It was also used in the Bible to speak of mending nets (Matthew 4:21). The idea is that of restoring something to its former condition for the purpose of being used.

A Sure Delight

James says that the restoration of a fallen Christian **shall save a soul from death, and shall hide a multitude of sins. (James 5:20)** The word death is used several ways in Scripture. There is spiritual death which is the state of every unsaved person (Ephesians 2:1; 2:5, 1 John 5:12). There is the second death which is eternal punishment in the lake of fire (2 Thessalonians 1:9, Revelation 21:8). Then there is physical death(1 Corinthians 15:21-22; Hebrews 9:27). It is the latter that James is referring to here in our text. The word of God clearly teaches that a believer who falls away and backslides may face death. As we learned earlier, John called it the **sin unto death (1 John 5:16-17)**. James is telling us that if we will invest ourselves in others, even the fallen, that some will repent and return to Christ avoiding premature death. James goes on to say, **and shall hide a multitude of sins.** When the backslider confesses the error of his way and returns to Christ, his sin is forgiven and washed away by the blood of our Saviour. **If we confess our sins, he is faithful and just to forgive us our sins, and to cleanse us from all unrighteousness. (1 John 1:9)** What an important and eternal work—the work of restoration.

www.ingramcontent.com/pod-product-compliance
Lightning Source LLC
Chambersburg PA
CBHW061942070426
42450CB00007BA/1029